To Betsy,
So darn proud of you!
THANK you for your
Purposefulness. :)

PRAISE FOR THE PURPOSEFUL MILLIONAIRE

"More now than ever, our nation needs James' positive message of self-mastery, positivity, and achievement. *The Purposeful Millionaire* is a powerful demonstration of James' journey toward the American Dream, as well as a toolkit for others to learn from. My hope is that anyone aspiring to be more, do more, and live more will read and glean knowledge from this book's inspirational words."

–United States Congresswoman,
Eddie Bernice Johnson

"The words of a real practitioner ring more true than any expert. James' success is priceless–he worked for it, earned it, and is gracious enough to share it."

–Javier Palomarez, President & CEO of the United
States Hispanic Chamber of Commerce (USHCC)

"James has been tremendously successful in business and in this book he shares some of the secrets to his success to inspire others to achieve their goals with the message that anyone can achieve greatness if they approach their goals with purpose."

–Nina Vaca, Chairman and CEO Pinnacle Group

"This well-written book offers impactful and insightful guidance to anyone who wants to get the most out of life. James represents the very best of the millennial generation. His guidance balances the wisdom of the ages with energy and enthusiasm. It offers straightforward yet impactful strategies for having a purposeful life."

–Joset Wright-Lacy, President, National Minority Supplier Development Council (NMSDC)

"Living a life on purpose is a key to having an abundant life. James hits the nail on the head in this powerful guide to making the most of life."

–David Osborn, Principal Owner of Keller-Williams and Author of Wealth Can't Wait

"James infuses everything he touches with his trademark blend of authenticity, optimism, and a celebration of diversity. He once told the NGLCC, 'Leaders succeed in business when they are honest, do not take shortcuts, and always travel the high road.' Having seen the fruits of James' commitment to helping others grow, I know the lessons put forth in *The Purposeful Millionaire* will help so many travel the high road to personal and financial success."

—Justin Nelson, Co-Founder & President, National Gay & Lesbian Chamber of Commerce (NGLCC)

"Mindset is everything! If you change your thinking, you change your habits thus changing your life and James reminds us of this in a beautifully simplistic way. This is a must read for anyone who needs a powerful reminder that the world is full of endless possibilities."

—Candace Waterman, Chief of Staff & Vice President, Women's Business Enterprise National Council (WBENC)

"Every adventure starts with the right equipment, and the *right guide*. In *The Purposeful Millionaire*, James shares his own adventures, returning with the tools, tactics and strategies to help you make it to the top in business and life. Stop searching in the dark. Pick up your copy of this dynamic guidebook today."

–Brad Szollose, TEDX Alum, Global Business Advisor, and Award-winning Author of Liquid Leadership

∾

"*The Purposeful Millionaire* is packed with important information and stories to help you achieve more, be more and live more fully. The key is having the emotional courage to look in the mirror and face your toughest opponent. James gives it to you straight. I highly recommend this book!"

–Sean Brawley, Coach Advisor to Pete Carroll, New York Yankees, and senior executives of GE, ITT and Creative Artists Agency

∾

"Don't misconstrue the title, this is not a 'get rich quick' book, but a true, practical and inspiring approach to success no matter what your career happens to be. Happiness is a choice and through his book, James shares his truths on achieving happiness and success – mind, body and spirit!"

–Terry Loftis, President, Eisenberg and Associates

"The Purposeful Millionaire changed my life! This book is a very easy read and you can feel James' personality throughout the book. These 52 rules have the potential to transform the life of everyone who reads it. Very well done!"

—Kimberly Beatty, Ed.D., Chief Academic Officer and Vice Chancellor, Houston Community College System

∽

"James is our 21st century Napoleon Hill. *The Purposeful Millionaire* is a powerful toolkit filled with tried and true success strategies reinvented for a modern world transformed by technology and driven by diversity. How fitting that he has produced a practical guidebook for those of us who have thirsted for timeless wisdom made even more relevant for our digital age."

—Anthony Shop, MBA, Co-Founder and Chief Strategy Officer, and Thomas Sanchez, President and CEO, Social Driver

∽

"James is a master of mindfulness and practical business wisdom. I highly recommend *The Purposeful Millionaire* to anyone who wants to deepen their life while achieving consistent commercial success."

—Tim Askew, CEO, Corporate Rain International and Author, The Poetry of Small Business

"This is more than motivational reading. It's a toolkit to change your life written by a man who is living proof of the truth of his philosophy."

—Mary Jennings (MJ) Hegar, Purple Heart Recipient and Author of Shoot Like a Girl

≈

"James shows us simple, yet extraordinarily profound and powerful thoughts and actions to effortlessly manifest happiness and wealth. His wisdom flows forth in this book and if you follow his suggestions your life will be the better for it."

—Marcia Martin, International Executive Coach, Trainer, and Co-Creator Transformational Leadership Council

≈

"James' triumph over near tragedy in *The Purposeful Millionaire* is A Must Read! He provides a timeless blueprint for success in a masterfully-written work of non-fiction that demonstrates how the "human will" provides the catalyst for extraordinary achievements. His 52 rules to success unlock the mystery to what is required and provides the plan-of-action that every person of every age and stage in life can follow to achieve their ultimate dream."

—Margaret Ford Fisher, Ed.D., President Houston Community College – Northeast

"As a successful physician with a disability, I found in James' book the very sort of practical suggestions that helped me achieve a professionally satisfying and financially rewarding career. I wish it had been available when I was starting out. I am pleased to know that other young career-minded disabled people will have *The Purposeful Millionaire* as a guidepost for their professional lives."

—Stanley K. Yarnell, M.D.

∽

"Knowing myself as well as the ropes of business are what have taken me the farthest in business. James' book is a clarion reminder of all that we can do, and all that we can become, so long as we nourish the subconscious with fodder for its greatest potential."

—Robert Grunnah, Managing Member, Penchant Capital

∽

"Happiness is measured by gratitude. Daily simple pleasures derive true happiness. *The Purposeful Millionaire* drives such virtues home with excellence and clarity."

—Lisa Harris, Managing Partner, Align Capital

"So much of what holds us back from reaching the dizzying heights we're each capable of is our limiting beliefs–of where we can go, of what we can have, of what we deserve. James provides a powerful personal story of transformation and a step-by-step guide to shifting this thinking–and our hearts–towards a future where we all can have prosperity and abundance beyond our wildest dreams. Don't miss this important message!"

–Jennifer Brown, Author of Inclusion: Diversity, the New Workplace, and the Will to Change

৵

"*The Purposeful Millionaire* is a great common sense business book. James explores the need for all of us to look in the mirror. In my career I've included small mirrors at my employees desks. These mirrors served multiple purposes: a reminder to smile when you answer the phone... smiling does make a difference and at times we can be our own worst enemy."

–Frank Veñegas, Jr., Chairman and CEO, Ideal Group

৵

"Define, focus, and reach your personal goals: James tells how in clear and eminently practical terms. His rules keep work and life in productive balance. Valuable counsel in our pressurized world!"

–Victor Rowley, J.D., Ph.D.

THE PURPOSEFUL
MILLIONAIRE

In order to get the full value of this book and to create the life you dream, you should visit:

www.PurposefulMillionaire.me/club-signup
and join The Purposeful Millionaire Club.

You will be provided with inspiration and powerful guidance that will take your personal and professional life to the next level.

And best of all, it's free!

A portion of the profit from this book will be dedicated to helping survivors of domestic violence.

To learn more, visit:
www.JamesNowlin.com/help-survivors

THE PURPOSEFUL MILLIONAIRE

52 RULES FOR CREATING A LIFE OF WEALTH AND HAPPINESS NOW

JAMES R. NOWLIN

For permission requests, write to the publisher, addressed "Attention: Permissions Coordinator," at the address below.

Purpose Driven Publishing
141 Weston Street, #155
Hartford, CT, 06141
www.PurposeDrivenPublishing.com

Ordering Information:
Quantity sales. Special discounts are available on quantity purchases by corporations, associations, and others. For details, contact the publisher at the address above.

Printed in the United States of America.

Edited by: Jake McDonie, Ph.D.
Cover design by: Jovincie Lizardo, graphic designer.
Cover photo: Ron Parks Photography.

ISBN-13: 978-1-946384-01-0
ISBN-10: 1-946384-01-1
Library of Congress Control Number: 2017936078

First edition, April 2017.

Purpose Driven Publishing helps non-fiction authors change the world, while growing their business, launching their speaking careers, and positioning themselves as thought leaders in their respective industries. Do you have a book idea you would like us to consider publishing? Please visit www.PurposeDrivenPublishing.com for more information.

This book is dedicated to every great educator who believed in me and pushed me, and among them all, Robert S. Brown, M.D., Ph.D. (Professor, University of Virginia School of Medicine), a titan of self-mastery who cares for me as a son, and Dean Sylvia Terry (University of Virginia), a shining force of nature who to this day inspires me to share my greatest gifts with the world.

CONTENTS

One can have no smaller or greater mastery than mastery of oneself.

–*Leonardo da Vinci*

FOREWORD

My Friend James—A Second Life, a Purposeful Life
By Tyler L. Cooke, M.D.

WHEN JAMES WAS granted a second life, he came back a different person. A near-death accident while I was kayaking with him on a lazy giant lake in East Texas at his lake house was a wake-up call that no one would wish upon another. My own journey spanned years traveling to some of the world's most remote and dangerous locations, including working for the Sea Shepherds in the Ross Sea of Antarctica. But I had one of my biggest scares not in the unruly Southern Ocean or a how-do-you-pronounce-that? village in the South Pacific, but with James on a fateful August day in 2012 when he nearly drowned in the midst of a harrowing storm.

We started that day with no hint of how it would later evolve. The air was calm, and we were catching up on each other's lives and mustering the energy to beat the summer heat by cooling off in the lake. We decided to go kayaking and as very experienced swimmers (I was a lifeguard in high school and enjoy surfing, and James had competed in triathlons), we left our life jackets at home and headed far out toward the middle of the lake, which in Texas size was more like a small sea. Then we slipped out for a swim, when seemingly out of nowhere, the sky turned a leaden gray, and fat rolling thunderclouds accompanied by a startlingly cold wind began whipping our faces. Before long, the placid lake had turned into a raging washing machine with whitecaps breaking over the top of our kayaks. Our boats quickly taking on water, we jumped back inside them and headed for the closest shoreline, but to no avail; our paddling was taking us nowhere, and the boats filled with water and sank.

We abandoned the sinking kayaks and swam but made little progress against the lake's lashings. I kept an eye on a point of reference on the shore and to my side to avoid swimming in circles, but that didn't seem to matter as we were literally going nowhere. The water was a whirlpool. Having been in the waters of Antarctica and surfed in some incredible weather conditions, I knew that we were in trouble. The water sustained its whirlpool grip. It was also dark outside now, which made it even harder for us to keep close to each other. Not that I was feeling in better control, but having been in this death trap of whitecaps crashing far above our heads for several minutes, I could tell that James had accidentally inhaled water and was in very bad shape. Every time I called out, he took longer to respond. I decided it was do-or-die time, so I put all my energy into survival mode, swimming more than a few hundred yards through the crashing waves to shore.

I screamed to him that I'd come back for him, all the while hoping that it wasn't too late for us and that I had made the right decision to separate from him. James promised me that he would survive.

As I made it within earshot of the shoreline, I yelled for help. Luckily a nearby resident heard me and launched his jet ski with me on the back holding a flashlight. Another neighbor dialed 911. Ambulances and rescuers were on the way. Thank goodness. But was it too late? A lot of time had passed, and I somehow had to get rid of the thought that we were returning to the water to recover James's dead body. I was determined to find my best friend—he had so much more to give to the world.

We intermittently killed the engine on the jet ski and called out for James to guide us to him, but we heard nothing in return for several minutes. With the fear of the worst spilling over me, I finally got a response, and we headed toward James's hardly audible call. We spotted him barely bobbing to the water's surface and mostly sinking below–we rushed to him. We pulled his limp body onto the back of the jet ski and I still remember the warm rush of what seemed like liters of dirty lake water being involuntarily vomited onto my feet. He had a pulse! *How had he survived near impossible odds?*

This man had been in the storm for a very long time, and there clearly wasn't much time before he would have died. As a physician, I know that people just don't inhale that amount of water into their lungs and struggle in that kind of storm for that length of time and survive. We rushed him to shore where a team of paramedics met us and rushed him to the hospital. With James still not in good shape and having taken on a tremendous amount of water, I was very concerned about the long-term outcome for him. He had obviously gone without oxygen for quite some time. In typical James fashion, though he was seconds from death, he fought during the storm and also while in the hospital. As James always did, he made good on his earlier promise—he had made it. He survived.

Unlike me, who was frightened beyond belief that day, James appreciates that day and calls it his second birth—his awakening. It reshaped his perspective for the better. He emerged more balanced in his approach to life, family, friends, business, relaxation, and his desire to give back to others. His confidence and steadfast determination behind growing his success as a businessman never wavered, but more items were included in the way he accounted for a total package of success in his life. He told others "I love you" much more, he meditated more, and he became incredibly purpose driven and appreciative of each new day. He made different priorities for his life and moved from Dallas to Austin for a better quality of life. He became a new man.

We all encounter potentially life-changing events. But the form they may take and whether or not we recognize them and make changes in the aftermath are another story. James was faced with his mortality and came out of it a better man, and I couldn't be more proud to call him my friend who is excited to share his path to success with you.

∽

I've known James Nowlin my entire adult life and have always believed that there was something different about him. From meeting him on our first day at the University of Virginia to witnessing his meteoric rise in business and life years later, I knew that James was always the guy who, if saying he was going to do something, would absolutely do it.

His rare personal qualities of flawless integrity and authenticity of character have distinguished him as a mentor, a teacher, a coach, and, moreover, a man whom people, including me, look up to, respect, and emulate. When James told me that he was writing *The Purposeful Millionaire* and asked me to write the foreword, I was immediately thrilled. Because James has such a compelling life story and an unshakable attitude geared for success, I thought there could be no better way for James to share his wisdom—his true gift—with the world.

Given the similarity of our upbringing it feels to me that James and I have known each other since birth. We first met as neighbors in the same dormitory (even then James somehow managed to be in charge–president of our dormitory!) at an elite university with less-than-privileged backgrounds trying to figure things out to make it on our own. We forged a bond through a tireless dedication to our studies, becoming familiar with all the best libraries on campus, lugging texts which, when piled, would often stack above our furrowed foreheads. The midnight oil would burn low in the late hours, but there was really no alternative for either of us. James and I were pioneers of our respective families. We were both among the first to leave home to attend college. There was no template to follow, no fallback if we faltered, and no cushion to soften any stumbling or lapses.

It was sometimes dizzying for me because I was young and as a teenager this was navigating uncharted territory, but there was also a comfort in going through the challenges with a friend who shared a similar position regarding success and dogged mindset. Prior to college, we had both worked hard to earn our successes and accomplishments to date but knew that the University of Virginia was the big leagues and that there was now significantly more on the line. There wasn't much glamor in those midnight oil moments, but they held hope and promise, and helped illuminate the still-somewhat-foggy path towards a rewarding future. Sure there were lighthearted, fun times, but both had the mindset that failure just wasn't an option so our studies always took priority.

No one other than the two of us would show us the way, other than ourselves, and over the years James would learn lessons about life and happiness that would center his core beliefs and validate his pathway to success. I would go on to become a neuroradiologist medical doctor, and James would go on to become... well, you already know that from reading the title of this book!

⚘

James lived to write this book. He is a living miracle, and I share his background with you so that you can clearly understand the gravity of what you are reading in your hands right now. James created himself. Nobody did that for him. It was James' mastery of self and his relationship with the universe that brought him to this level. Though circumstances were never ideal for him, he envisioned the idea, laid out the plan, and executed his dream to be a Purposeful Millionaire. That is why his book is important to this world, and is, as he calls it, a "tool for opening the mindset of opportunity" for all people who want more wealth and more happiness.

As a business leader and close adviser to powerful CEOs, James is proud to have achieved at the highest levels while living his core values authentically and not shrinking from his personal identity as a man of greatness who never forgot where he came from. James is unequivocally respected for the content of his character, his leadership qualities, and his expertise. People see him for who he is—intelligent, hard-working, and gracious.

If James can survive the literal waters from which he was pulled, he knows that you can survive and thrive in any kind of choppy waters of business or life that come your way. He knows how to navigate beautifully and damn-near flawlessly the most complex waters of business and life, which have turned great profits for him.

James knows himself, and he likes his truest, most authentic self, and people like that about him; in turn, he has been rewarded for such qualities. He knows the rules and plays by the rules. Life has not been easy for him, but he certainly makes it look easy. He wants you to learn from his mistakes so that the road is easier for you, and moreover, so that you may fully glean the rules of the game of wealth and happiness that he has laid out for you. That is what this book is all about.

As you read, know that the words of this book resonate from a man of great integrity, methodicalness, and character who has been humbled by this world, but who always finds a way to end up on top. James is the real deal. He has always been different from—or should I say better than—the circumstances that have shaped him. He envisions the world a better place with a greater distribution of the pies of wealth and happiness for those who want them—for those who are willing to do the work to gain them. His words are a plea to you. If you are ready, I am certain that you will find this book helpful as your own personal tool to becoming a Purposeful Millionaire.

THE SUCCESS FORMULA–
YOU CAN DO IT TOO!

AFTER I WAS pulled from that lake, I realized that my life needed to change. And I hope that you, without needing to have a near-death experience, might realize that your life can change too. If you are ready, I want your wake-up call to come right now with the fifty-two rules of this book.

Like my former self, you may not be living up to your highest potential, and you may not currently be doing the work to master yourself, and thus your universe. In my previous life, though I had "succeeded" by most folks' measures, I was not open to receiving the full abundance of the universe. I cannot honestly say that I lived each day with profound purpose, nor did I understand the discipline required to do so or the joy received from doing so.

But my life changed for the better after that day on the lake. Today, I know that the worst thing in the world is the difference between who we are and what we could have become. That is precisely why I charted a new, purposeful course for my life and wrote this book, the inspiration for which came when I was granted a fully-awakened second life. My life today is a new one.

It is fundamentally different from the way it once was, and I have purposefully set out on fulfilling my highest potential. My life is now filled with more opportunity, fulfillment, and excitement than I ever imagined. But getting here was not easy.

As recounted by my dear friend in the Foreword, in the late summer of 2012, when my half-dead body was pulled from a storm in the middle of an East Texas lake, I had a real wake-up call. After I regained full consciousness, the first words that the doctor said to me, with a smile on his face, were, "Guess what. You are a miracle. I have worked on this lake for a long time, and one thing is certain—nobody really survives drownings like the one you went through. Welcome back." I could not fully grasp what he said at the time, but I will never forget his words.

Weeks later, after my health had rebounded, and my lungs, which had been filled with bacteria-ridden lake water, had healed, I regained the mental sharpness that I had lost from being deprived of oxygen during the drowning, my vocabulary improved, and I would reflect each day on the questions: *Had I lived purposefully? Had I mattered? Had I been completely open to receiving the full abundance of the universe?* Sadly, the answer was "no." But I knew that the drowning could be a turning point for me and an opportunity for a greater life if I focused on using my mind as a tool to get greater success and happiness out of life. After the shock of the incident had settled, each day of my life going forward I made a promise to myself that I would do everything I could to answer those questions with a resounding "Yes!"

With each passing day, it sunk in more and more that I was a living miracle. With that realization, I vowed never to waste another day of my life living up to less than my full potential. Because of that commitment, my consciousness of the world would become less superficial and arrive from a significantly deeper place, and my relationship with the universe would be taken to a higher level. I knew that, yes, I could indeed have it all *and* enjoy each step of the journey.

Because of my awakening, I am grateful for that fateful day in the water, for it taught me how to live better and think in terms of abundance and fulfillment, without limitation. It taught me that I could have everything I wanted in life so long as I overcame my self-limiting beliefs. Previously, I had thought that working hard, traveling to exotic places, having flashy friends, and buying expensive toys were what I should do to live purposefully, or at a bare minimum to look the part of a success story. But inside, though I was a success story, I was somewhat empty and far from purpose-driven.

Though you would not know it from looking at me from the outside, I was living a stressed-out, unexamined life, and was achieving less than my potential. On a happiness scale of one to ten, I probably would have found myself stuck somewhere between a five and an eight on any given day. Looking back on that life, it kind of sucked. I was without deep-rooted purpose despite some of my natural characteristics as a good businessman, loving family man, kind person, and skilled networker. Making the change from a respectable but ho-hum existence to a more meaningful and powerful one was difficult. Why? you may ask. Because unless the mind is trained to think in terms of radical expansion and abundance, the mind will allow self-doubt and fear to be in control. Getting to that positive mindset was a seismic shift for me. But I knew that I was extremely lucky to have a second chance at life and that this time around, I had to live a more examined life, a more abundant life, and a more purposeful life.

The Purposeful Millionaire, though not an autobiography, is about my journey, which has at times humbled me to my knees. This book's words are so powerful because the knowledge that I have been blessed with, or earned, I should say, arrive from having experienced the right amount of pain and suffering as well as the right amount of success. This book is about the hard-knock lessons that I learned along the way to achieving a life of abundance and true happiness. To get to that newfound greater joy in my life as well as to a greater station of wealth, I have not hidden from anything about myself or from the gifts with which I have been blessed. I promised myself that I would not squander or underuse my unique talents, for they are my gifts to the world and the universe's charge for me. My journey through this process helped me to face my truths to become the person that I am today. At my core, I am happy, authentic, and unapologetic about all of who I am—including being a self-made, very financially successful man.

To get to those greater riches as well as a greater self, complete authenticity has been key. Knowing myself, accepting myself, being true to myself, and loving myself have done more than just benefitted me personally: it has swung open the doors for others to genuinely like and trust me in business. In turn, some of these people have endowed great responsibility upon me in my business and personal affairs. People are attracted to others who exude this kind of exceptional energy, self-love, and authenticity. Such characteristics render a person magnetic. Others cannot help but want to do business with a man who believes in himself. No one wants to do business with someone who is full of self-doubt or marked by weakness of character.

I knew that I had to master love of myself before I ever worked on attempting to achieve my full potential. One thing I am certain about is that if I am leading a boardroom meeting and my mind subconsciously focuses on how different I am from the people in the room (they are usually much older and of a different race), instead of the much more critical matters at hand, I become the victim of self-diminishing thoughts and my effectiveness dwindles. And though most identity categories should never matter in business, I also happen to be what some folks categorize as a double minority: I am both black and gay. But those social boxes are only a very small part of who I am, and I certainly do not allow them to limit me. Because such social boxes, or any other categories such as gender, socioeconomic status, level of education, class, and so on can create mental roadblocks in people or subconsciously occupy space in their minds, I knew that I first had to be completely comfortable with myself and value myself.

I, like every human being, have at one time or another played victim to self-minimizing thoughts that I permitted to be planted into my head. Such parasitic thoughts never lead to a change in circumstances. As you read this book, use it as a tool to wash your mind clear of old baggage, negative ways of thinking, and self-doubt. You are better than that way of thinking.

Though I learned to master my mind mostly by trial and error, once I finally figured out things, I felt awakened. My journey of self-mastery has made me feel not just powerful, but uniquely so. I realized that many other people on this earth never attain true success (or happiness, for that matter), so this book is my testimonial for spreading the good news of what this kind of self-love can do for others. If I can overcome all of my hang-ups and achieve not only financial success but also an exquisitely purposeful life filled with joy, deeper consciousness, and self-love, then you can too!

I write to help you tap into your inner greatness to achieve your goals. Along the way I might sound a little preachy, but that's what a good coach does—he preaches, he teaches, he repeats himself, he shares, he explains the rules, he leads by example, and he motivates because he wants others to succeed. This book is your coach, your manual, your tool to help you study yourself under a microscope. By doing so, you will find out what is holding you back.

I lay out easy, practical rules in this book for you to apply to your life. We dig deep into a special formula to achieve success, shining a light on exactly what you should and should *not* do to succeed. Taking the advice is up to you. If you take the formula and the words of this book seriously, by learning, reflecting upon, and growing as you read, you will come closer to mastering your consciousness, and thus your inner power to become both wealthier and happier.

When it comes to becoming both wealthy and happy, it is important to understand that while some people ask for abundance and happiness, others do not—or better yet, they do not know how to ask for it. They would rather complain about the raw deal that life has handed them. The formula for achievement that will further advance you beyond those individuals is simple. Once you have an idea and ask the universe for that idea to come to fruition, you must make a plan and then execute that plan. As such, the formula for the journey to greater wealth and happiness looks like this:

Idea + Plan + Execution (90 percent of your time) = Success

Or, in other words…

Inspiration + Preparation + Perspiration (90 percent of your time) = Elevation

This recipe for success is so powerful and relevant that I have broken down the book into four component parts: Idea, Plan, Execution, and Success. Intentionally, the "Idea" section of the book is the shortest because everyone has ideas and they are easy to come by. The "Plan" section is ever so slightly longer because in life as well as in business, plans change—having the discipline to maintain consistent behaviors and systems is far better; and the "Execution" section is the lengthiest because this phase takes longer and requires far more work than its two preceding phases. These three component parts of the formula lead us to what we all want, "Success." This final part of the book expresses the beautiful culmination of abundance, happiness, purposefulness, consciousness, self-love, and joy; it also explains how to sustain these things in your life and to build upon them. You will eventually achieve nothing less than success if you do the required work in the first three sections of the book.

As you read through all four parts, it is important to note that the goal of this book is *not* to provide you with the exact idea or plan for how to achieve happiness and success for yourself, but rather to give you the mindset and thought process that you need to figure out what unique idea and plan are right for you. I certainly do not have a monopoly on ideas or plans. Knowing that, the purpose of this book is to not force anything on you but, rather, to coach you to become a master of yourself so that you can apply the formula for success. Money should not be made by imitation but as an outcome of one's uniqueness. Don't compete—be unique. If you read this book closely and do the Purposeful Millionaire Power Play exercises at the end of each chapter, the idea and plan will most certainly come to you.

Now that you have a better understanding of how this book and the formula of *Idea + Plan + Execution = Success* will work in your life, understand that you have something very special to work with that many others will never have or take the time to learn. Most people are never taught how to achieve wealth or happiness and end up going through years, sometimes decades, of spinning their wheels and ultimately failing. Such failure creates a life of regret. I certainly don't want you to be like most people. I want you to be so much more, and I want the journey to be easier for you. The application of the formula in all that you do in your daily affairs is about mastering your greatest tool, the mind, which will lead to mastery of your soul, your wallet, and your destiny.

As your coach, I am going to push you and ask a lot of you in this book so that you can do the work to become a Purposeful Millionaire, or at a minimum, so that you can heighten your consciousness, also known as your mindfulness. The Purposeful Millionaire Power Play exercises at the end of each chapter will help you to evaluate your life and prepare your mind for greater potential. Grab your pad and pencil and do them, scribble notes all throughout the book, dog-ear pages that have a special meaning to you, and revisit pages that motivate you. Invest in yourself, and use this book as a guide for lifting yourself to higher ground. You will be glad you did.

As you read, you will find many of my favorite inspirational quotes from all different kinds of people as a means for you to learn and tap into the unequivocal power of your consciousness. Each quote is by someone who has made a powerful contribution to the world and who has mastered his or her life in one way or another. Each quote should remind you that the thoughts and rules in this book did not all originate with me and are not mine alone to share with you but, rather, that you are in the company of greatness throughout your journey. My hope is that you will find some quotation or nugget of truth that will not only stick with you, but will uplift, encourage, and ignite your passion for achieving your dreams.

Get ready to journey through a personal adventure to find your higher purpose, to learn the rules of the game of success, and to maximize your experience on this planet by living an epic, powerful, abundant life. This is my second life, and this book is my gift to you. Dare to believe in yourself more than you ever have, do the work, and join me in being a Purposeful Millionaire!

PART I
THE IDEA
IDEA + PLAN + EXECUTION = SUCCESS

CHAPTER ONE

I WANT TO BE RICH

In reading the lives of great men, I found that the first victory they won was over themselves. [S]elf-discipline with all of them came first.

—*Harry S. Truman*

"I WANT TO be rich." When I was a kid, that was exactly what I said when adults asked me what I wanted to be when I grew up. Not expecting that response, some of them laughed. Others tried to clarify the question by correcting me and then asking me what profession I wanted to pursue. Unlike most young boys who said that they wanted to be firefighters or doctors, I simply repeated, "I want to be rich." For the life of me, I most certainly did not want to be poor. Never ever. Being poor stinks, and I had had my taste of plenty of arguments about money in my household while I was growing up, though publicly we put on the image that we had plenty of it. At an early age, I somehow thought that wealth could make those arguments magically go away. Though I was not entirely correct about that assumption, I learned later in life that proper care and management of money and one's subconscious could make life a whole lot easier.

My humble beginnings only reinforce the importance of money. I am proud that I grew up in the Blue Ridge Mountain foothills of southern Virginia as a black kid in a town called *Lynch*burg of all places–go figure. My father began his career at UPS as a package delivery driver and was later promoted to a tractor-trailer driver. He had a good stable job and was a dues-paying member of a labor union. My mother was a factory worker at the highest-paying plant in the region for more than a decade and later got laid off. She then went on to work part-time and put herself through college while I was in high school so that she could become a public school teacher.

I admired my parents' work ethic. By Lynchburg standards, they had made it. They worked hard and expected the same from my sister and me. Life was work, and work was expected to be done without any questions asked. In our house, work we understood, but money was an entirely different matter. Nonetheless, what I heard and saw at a young age as my parents constantly fought about money caused me to take a great interest in learning more about it.

Trying to keep up with the Joneses ate us alive. My father wanted us to *be* the Joneses and would go to all lengths to achieve status and admiration from others. My family lived this way for the entire seventeen years I lived in my father's house. We had lots of things: an 1800-square-foot colonial ranch style home with stately Doric columns and a tricked-out basement, tractors, a timeshare for a vacation property, a shiny red van with shag carpet and a sofa in the back that flipped down into a bed with the touch of a button, an old mule-like horse named Blossom that was as mean as a rattlesnake (in fact, the horse was so mean that she bit me one day—I have the scar tissue on my chest to prove it. But heck, we had a horse and no one else around us did!), sixty-five acres of land, and nice furniture and clothes. These material things gave us public credence. However, funds for education, self-uplift, and other critical expenses were never a priority. Our household embraced a *poverty consciousness*, which is a feeling and value system associated with a fear of material and financial lack, and an almost religious belief in limitation. This kind of thinking tangles the mind in the material world of believing that one always needs more *things* and more money with which to buy them, in order to be happy. In such a trap, one's awareness is focused on want and not on appreciation. This impoverished thinking enslaves minds, confuses material trappings with happiness, and blinds one's outlook on life. A toxic cycle of worry regarding future security ultimately manifests itself as a lack of financial abundance. In poverty consciousness, nothing is ever enough. In our home, we may have not known the fancy definition for our value system, but it was surely how we lived, and thus how I learned to think about the world as a child.

My father was the nominal leader of our house, but he was not a very good one at that. Through his own miseducation and his mismanagement of earnings, we were forced to keep up public appearances of living the American dream without the means to do so. Keeping up a dog and pony show of pretending to be rich was draining for each of us, especially my mother. In that small town, everyone knew everyone else as well as everyone else's business. My mother tried her hardest to keep up the appearance of happiness in public, but when at home, she lived in fear of a slap across the face, a busted lip, a black eye, a dinner plate thrown across the room, a knock to the floor, or much worse from my father if we ever ran out of money for one of his personal pursuits or other interests. She did her best to protect herself and her children from harm but did not always succeed.

Though my hope is that my father is a different man today, his altercations about money were tempered by his intense insecurities, particularly when he was under the frequent influence of alcohol. I—my sister as well, though she strived to be daddy's girl—lived in fear of the possibilities of what he would emotionally or physically do to us when the stresses of the world were too much for him to handle. Lights on, lights off: that's how we read him, and we had best know how to gauge his mercurial temper. Otherwise, we faced battle and his favorite verbal promise that he would "hospitalize" us or our mother. On more than a few occassions he beat the daylights out of us and always sealed each event with the finger-in-your-face promise of, "I will hospitalize you next time."

All those issues aside, most of the problems of my parents' marriage, including my father's flagrant adultery and frequent nights spent at his mistresses' homes (most of whom I met and knew as a child), were not secrets but more like conditions that we were expected to accept privately and never mention publicly. We were the Nowlins and had an *image* to uphold publicly, of course. Our mess of private problems were unfortunately sharpened like a razor because of my father's obsession with money and his burning desire for status and special recognition—and boy did he love to brag! How could this nightmare within our household have been created by money and one man's insecurities? I would not learn the answer to that question until I left home to attend college.

Rule #1: First love yourself, and the universe will conspire to lift you higher. Your thoughts about yourself, money, and what other people think about you—and the way you respond to those thoughts—can build you up or completely tear you down.

When I arrived at The University of Virginia (UVA) at seventeen, I learned that my family's public Lynchburg image was a complete charade. Prior to attending college, I thought family civility was only something to be watched on Friday night sitcoms. As unrealistic as I thought those families were, they made me dream of living like them one day. No fear. No horrible dysfunction and physical altercations. Just relative decency and civility with a dose of healthy determination to deal with any challenges that came their way. Wow, what a novel concept! I, on the other hand, had survived living with a father who was dangerous because of his love of money, yearning for control, and a need to keep up appearances. Deep within him was a horrible, gremlin-like saboteur that caused his children to be ignored while he splurged on things that neighbors, friends, extended family, and the public would see: the big house, the land, the fishing boat, the flashy van, the ragtag horse. Perhaps he thought that if he dazzled others with his lifestyle, they would accept, like, or even love him. He was a wonderfully charming soul in public–a monster behind the four walls of our house. Whatever the case, a lack of self-love was at the tragic core of the demon.

Though my mother somehow still loved that man intensely, she would muster the courage to escape the self-esteem-reducing entanglement of a twenty-seven-year marriage of private, devastating physical and emotional abuse. She divorced him when I was in law school, got her own place, and though he begged her to come back and promised to change, she was resolute. With the divorce, my father lost his family and gained the judgment of the small town's critical eye. He would later go on to remarry and subsequently find himself spending a stint in jail for a domestic violence act with his second wife. The public charade had been fully exposed. The guy with the big house was apparently not so perfect after all. I admire my mother for many things, but the courage to grow her own legs, walk away, and stay away is what I will always admire the most about her. She now lives a dignified life filled with peace, joy, self-respect, fulfilling employment at the corporation for which I am CEO, and is financially independent with the freedom to come and go as she pleases—a life of blessings and greatness indeed. She shares her love, joy, and earned wisdom with others, and now holds her head high in public with absolute authenticity and pride.

> Your greatness is limited only by the investments you make in yourself.
>
> —*Grant Cardone*

Today, I am grateful for the lessons that my father's saboteur would teach me, for I would learn from them, allow them to serve as the foundation for my inner drive, and chart my course for a much different life full of self-love and abundance. Most importantly, I would learn from that saboteur what *not* to do. My journey to strip myself of a consciousness of abuse and poverty has done me more good than I will ever be able to measure. As I became my own man, I would release all old wounds and pray for the healing of my father's soul. Instead of using the poverty consciousness and unsteadiness of my upbringing as a sob story, I use it as a tool that motivates me. Those seventeen years in that stately but broken house on the hill built character and a determination to not accept certain circumstances as the truth or as the boundaries of my future reality. Thank you for that, universe!

I am fortunate that not all of my formative experiences happened in my childhood home. At university, where I was exposed to middle-class students whose families genuinely seemed to value education in addition to students from generationally-moneyed families, my young mind quickly associated their lifestyles with civility, poise, respect, dignity, and quiet indoor voices. They were classy. Though some of these students' families were likely far from perfect, I would observe them while reflecting on my own family experiences, and so create my own muse, stare into its eyes, and set out to create a good honest life for myself.

A key turning point for me came one day when I overheard one of my roommates talking to his parents on the phone. After he had thanked them for the check that they had overnighted to him to purchase additional books for a course that he wished to audit, he ended the conversation with, "I love you, Mom. I love you, Dad. Thank you so much. Talk to you next week." Holy cow! "I love you"? What kind of language was this kid speaking? He not only got a check and was encouraged to audit a course that piqued his interest but also told his parents, "I love you." For the life of me, I had never heard so many positive things going on in one family conversation, and we had not said or heard those three extraordinarily powerful words when I was growing up. No checks, affirmations of "I love you," extra books, or encouragement for me. But we certainly had a big house, full liquor cabinets to entertain, and a ragtag horse that graced our front yard.

A few days later, I called my mom and though I knew that I would not be receiving a check from my parents for anything (thank goodness for eventual employment as a resident assistant by Student Affairs to pay for my housing, partial scholarships, and Sallie Mae, the student loan company that I would use to finance my education), I politely asked her that we start something new: we would end every phone conversation with "I love you." It was just as awkward as could be for the first year or so to say those words, and we forgot to do so at times. But by modeling more functional families, I began a tradition within ours for us to show more love and appreciation to one another. This "I love you" communication would be the foundation upon which I would continue emulating the behaviors of other students and their families whom I saw as both highly functional and financially successful. The next four years at UVA would serve as a magical experiment of observation and emulation. I would work on erasing self-defeating thoughts and actions along with the poverty consciousness with which I had been endowed, while constructing a new conscience anchored in self-love, love of others, respectful communication, financial literacy, money management, goal-setting, and appreciation for opportunity.

After UVA, a self-aborted year at Howard University College of Medicine (thank you Howard for the full scholarship), three years at Duke Law (thank you Duke for the partial scholarship), initiation into the State Bar of Texas, and a stint as a corporate attorney turned businessman, I would learn more meaningful lessons about what wealth and happiness were all about—how wealth discriminated against those who merely talked about it as well as how it also seemed to be attracted to those who knew how to act upon it.

Here are some of the basic principles of the game of wealth creation and happiness that I have learned on my journey that I want to share with you. I live by them. Read them and reread them until you understand them. These principles are foundational to your greater understanding of the fifty-two rules of wealth and happiness throughout the rest of this book.

Thoughts and Mindset

1. Money is attracted to people who possess certainty and purposefulness.

2. It never occurs to most people that they can become wealthy.

3. Most people do not simply decide to be wealthy. Wealth is a choice. To achieve it requires specific action. But it is a choice that is available to almost everyone.

4. People spend time with folks with whom they feel most comfortable. The people around us help to create our mindset and opportunities. By changing our net-work, we can change our net-worth.

5. Money will not make you happy, especially if your value system is compromised.

6. To think like a self-made wealthy person, you must look at wealth in terms of time and freedom.

7. Most folks think in terms of short-term, fast, easy gains. They are willing to spend more time playing the lottery—configuring strategies for the right lucky numbers—than doing the hard, day-to-day work over many years that creates most wealth.

8. Self-made wealthy people have enterprise mindsets and think in terms of scaling their enterprises so that others do the work, not in terms of individual tasks or billable hours, both of which have limits.

9. Get to know who you are, and never compromise your value system. The higher you go, the more your values will be tested.

10. Be careful whom you choose as mentors.

Discipline and Habits

1. Discipline and routine may be boring, but by golly, those two things have created empires.

2. Most people fail to ever exploit their God-given gifts.

3. Chip away at your plan every single day, and before you know it, you will have a priceless sculpture.

4. Successful people are not just lucky; they are disciplined. They have habits, rituals, and mindsets that brought about their success.

5. Discipline is difficult. Frugality, delayed gratification, and the execution of long-term strategy are not easy, but they are all achievable.

6. Procrastination is the killer of all dreams. You will never be younger than you are today, so why not start executing your plan right now?

7. A few minutes of self-directed love, deep breathing, and meditation each day will change your life.

8. Go deep, not wide, with what you are good at and sell it. It is usually very complex, challenging for others to do well, or simply not a talent of most other people.

9. In the game of success, you get one point for an idea, nine points for a plan, and ninety points for execution. Most folks get stuck in the idea phase or the planning phase. It is only when you do all three things that you achieve success.

10. Act now. You are running out of time. Achieving the dream and driving a Bentley (or being driven in one) at the age of forty-five surely has to be a lot more fun than pinching pennies your entire life to save and drive one at seventy-five.

Attitude and Expectations

1. Your circumstances must not be your thoughts.

2. You are not one vacation or one retirement away from happiness. Your mind controls your happiness. Happiness can already be right here, right now.

3. Leadership should be honed and treasured. Help to pull up people around you, and you will be lifted higher. Leadership is not about being bossy or being a jerk.

4. Always avoid cheap things (they will not last), cheap people (they undervalue the efforts and contributions of others), and shortcuts (they usually do not work in the long haul).

5. Never mistake wealth for wisdom.

6. Common sense is not so common. Take advantage of that fact and the marketplace will reward you.

7. The world does not care two cents about your effort. The world only cares about results.

8. The marketplace will usually pay you what you are worth. If you want to earn more, you must learn more.

9. If you dream small, you will live small. Many people are committed to achieving little dreams. Achieving little dreams sometimes takes just as much work as big dreams. So why not dream big?

10. Always think in terms of abundance and increase, not decrease or lack. Think in terms of lack, and you will lack.

11. Be willing to shake up your posse. The people closest to you are a perfect reflection of exactly who you are and exactly what you will be.

12. Always stay hungry.

Humility and Kindness

1. Pray or meditate daily for your abundance—an increase to your health, wealth, wisdom, happiness, family, and like-minded friends.

2. Family must always come before things. Being wealthy and lonely is tantamount to misery. There are many people who so suffer.

3. Be outgoing and kind to everyone. Give folks the benefit of the doubt, and always stay positive.

4. Stay humble and be grateful.

5. Genuinely acknowledge and celebrate each and every blessing that comes your way—even the small ones.

All of these principles were learned over time but first began with a seismic shift in my mindset in my early years. The shift came by way of my exposing myself to people who had achieved at higher levels than me. I observed their habits. I took mental notes on everything they did from how they tied their shoes to how they compartmentalized their time to how they processed certain issues. On a daily basis, all of these learnings fed my subconscious the fuel that it needed for a mindset of abundance, appreciation, and happiness. These thoughts are with me and cannot be taken from me. That is why I can breathe each day with the confidence that regardless of my future circumstances, every day of my life going forward will be better than the last.

As a kid, I imagined wealth to be possible one day perhaps if I were extremely lucky and some kind of divine intervention occurred. But at a bare minimum, even if there would never be a lottery windfall or inheritance, I was certain that I would manage what money I made well enough not to fight within my home about it. That lesson in particular, to its core, had been learned and was a great starting point for me. Over the years I would learn so many more valuable lessons. I had cleared the right pathway for a consciousness of achievement and abundance and had done so at a relatively young age. Though I had not been taught this way of thinking, I knew that my life was now changed forever. And for that, I am grateful. Now my duty is to share that way of thinking with you.

PURPOSEFUL MILLIONAIRE POWER PLAY

1. Each person's life is the result of his or her experiences, particularly formative childhood experiences. Reflect upon the beliefs about money that you were taught by the people who raised you. Did they believe that they could pinch pennies or save their way into wealth? Did they blame rich people or politics for their problems? Were they shopaholics who filled an emotional void by buying things or hoarding? Are you like them or completely different from them? Did they fight within the household about differing monetary value systems or practices? Did miseducation and fighting about money interfere with their quality of life?

   a. Write a two to three paragraph letter to yourself about how you will break this cycle of misuse or abuse of money, miseducation about money, or self-defeating attitudes about money.

   b. Write a two to three paragraph letter to the person or people who taught you bad habits about money and forgive them. Keep this letter locked in your files, or destroy it if you like. There is no need to mail the letter unless you wish to do so. The letter is for your own personal healing, not for the other person or people.

2. Self-made rich people think and approach the world entirely differently from other people. Reread the rules of how wealthy people think under, "Thoughts and Mindset," "Discipline and Habits," "Attitude and Expectations," "Humility and Kindness," and reflect upon whether your value system is consistent with these principles. Be honest with yourself, and make a list of rules that you are not living up to so that you can make immediate changes to your mindset.

3. Repeat out loud five times, "I have everything that it takes to be healthy, wealthy, and happy. I am a Purposeful Millionaire."

CHAPTER TWO

I WANT TO BE MORE

Live life as if everything is rigged in your favor.

—*Rumi*

I CANNOT HELP but cry tears of joy when I reflect on the long-term outcome of the courageous idea to walk away from my practice as a first-year twenty-six-year-old corporate attorney at one of Texas's top law firms. This audacious decision would later become the launchpad for my professional and personal successes for years to come. Although I was layered early on with the material and ego-based trappings that come with being a young man with a healthy six-figure salary, benefits galore, and a floor-to-ceiling glass office atop one of Dallas's most striking skyscrapers, a voice inside my head told me to walk away. And so I did. I had found the practice of corporate law quite unfulfilling. I also despised my boss who had driven me to feel that way. He had told me on more than one occasion his displeasure with the firm's commitment to diversity recruitment (which in effect had meant hiring me), and though he liked the work that I was doing and had once told me that I was smart, he did not like or respect me as a person. His words hurt me to my core.

One day in front of another senior partner, with glaring eyes my boss shouted at me and told me that if I screwed up a particular legal document that I was drafting for him, he would *fire me on the spot*. Shocked at his public affirmation and coldness about the future of my career, the other partner who overheard him walked into my office the next day, closed the door, and asked me, "Does he always talk to you that way?" I confided that he did and broke down into tears. The bullying had been going on since I started at the firm. I explained to the senior partner that my boss had professed his displeasure with having not only a black associate working for him but, moreover, one who was, in his words, of the *gay lifestyle*. This was 2007. This job was my very first as an attorney and there were not a whole lot of rights or protections back then for people who had the integrity and guts to not closet their true identities, particularly in the workplace.

The abuse continued, and I went to work each day scared for my future, allowing my boss to dig for me a grave of self-hatred and fear. He would tell me to lock myself in my office and get my work done. He would say, "Make sure my clients don't find out about you." Each day working for him tore at my soul a little more, leaving me more confused, more voiceless, more purposeless. In the confines of the parking lot before walking into the tower in the morning, I would sometimes vomit. In the halls of the firm, I would smile when others greeted me and pretend that everything was okay. That was me at one of my most unhappy, inauthentic times in life. But I was my mother's son and somehow found the courage to walk out one day and not return. I quit.

No label, no slogan, no party, no skin color, and indeed no religion is more important than the human being.

–James Baldwin

In the months to come, after walking out on an abusive boss, with the affirming and unconditional support of my life partner, John, I subsequently started my own corporate consulting firm, a shop that I named Excel Global Partners. The very idea of Excel Global Partners and its potential would reset my focus and, better yet, my confidence. In the beginning months of being my own boss, I found peace in not having to answer to the old xenophobe back at the law firm. I could breathe. But little did I know at the time, more challenges would ensue. The launch of Excel Global Partners would coincide with an event that the world would later call The Great Recession, the worst economic downturn that our nation had seen in generations. I had thought, "Boy am I lucky! I had the courage to leave the mental abuse of a boss, only to be smacked with a downward spiraling economy that had seemed just fine six months prior." My timing could not have been worse. With no clients, little money saved for bills, and only an inkling of an idea about how to build my own business, my self-esteem was back in the dumps. Also during that time, John was severed from his job as the young CFO of a large global company during their buy-out by a private equity group. We had gone from the high six figures to zero figures, with a mountain of student debt and bills galore in desperate need of pay.

During that dark period, we were not alone. Some of our friends lost their homes. Some were forced to declare bankruptcy, and others lost every scintilla of hope that they once had in the American Dream. This time in our nation stunk. Feeling disenfranchised and humiliated was demoralizing to us all. The wrath of that stalemated global economy held back no punches, particularly to young folks like my friends and me who were just getting on their feet while weighed down with massive law school and college debt. It was not a joyous time for any of us, but looking back on that experience, I know that each bad day fundamentally changed something about us.

The myopia and poverty consciousness that I had been taught as a child somehow reminded me that my hard work and education would never pay off but rather leave me shackled with debt from higher learning. Fear constantly crept through my mind. *Would I survive? Would I lose my home too? Had I made the biggest mistake of my life by leaving the financial comforts of a top law firm to pursue my dream of being independent and freed from the shackles of boss abuse?*

Those thoughts stayed front and center during each agonizing and headache-filled day for me. I had to do something to survive, and I was determined that that economy would not get the best of me. Though that period of global economic horror rocked my world, the outcome of it was that it made me pretty damn tough: more strategic, more financially conservative, more disciplined, and less arrogant. As a youngster, my eyes opened not only to the unpredictability of the world in which we live but also, as I would discover, to a world of significantly greater opportunity. When I reflect on the fright of those years and how they equipped me to tap into my inner courage as well as to find my gold, I cannot help but weep tears of joy and appreciation. You may have been right there with me, going through something similar in your life too. But I must say that as I look back on the experience, I am grateful that I got over my fears and frustrations. The universe was making me tougher and preparing me for so much more.

Rule #2: Take the first step. You will never have an amazing journey if you do not take the first step, even if doing so scares the daylights out of you.

Just as I discovered when I walked away from my legal career, the first step in changing your life will be the most courageous step. Each step after that gets a little easier as you face your fears and gain confidence coupled with the knowledge that everything is going to be all right. With no guaranteed future income, lots of bills to be paid, and just an idea of what I wanted my life to look like, I found that my choice to leave the practice of law to start my own gig equipped me with a rawness, a drive to succeed, and a practicality that I had never had before. My short-lived career up to that point had represented more than the six-figure salary. It was a symbol that I had made it. I was still just a twenty-something-year-old kid who had grown up in the rural hills of Virginia. I had found myself in the big city working on one of the top floors of a beautiful tower in Dallas—Big D—the land of big dreams, big buildings, big personalities, and big highways. I was thriving, but I knew within me that regardless of the numbers written on my paycheck, I deserved to be respected as a human being, at a minimum, and that I was meant for so much more.

Faith is taking the first step even when you don't see the whole staircase.

—Dr. Martin Luther King, Jr.

Riddled with doubt and insecurities, I continued to question my decision to leave my practice. I doubted and questioned myself, *Was I about to throw it all away just because I couldn't get along with a boss? Was I not strong enough to effectively fight back at that xenophobe? Did I lack courage by not staying? Was I running from something?*

All I knew at the time was that I was a beacon of hope back home in little 'ole Lynchburg. I was the first in the family to earn a doctorate degree or make it to the big white-collar leagues. It felt nice. Folks looked up to me, and I was relatively aware of that. I felt their love and prayers from afar and still do to this day. I had made it, and they were all watching me to see if I would rise or stumble or, worse yet, fall on my face. I was so afraid of failing as I took the first step by leaving the law firm to protect my sanity, my well-being, and my self-respect.

> If you want something you've never had, then
> you have to do something you've never done and
> sometimes go after something you have never seen.
>
> —*Unknown*

Today, as I look back on that frightening decision—the first step in changing my life by leaving my law practice—I feel grateful for the strength that I found within my young self to leave. I know now that things did not happen *to* me. They happened *for* me.

Fast forward a little more than a decade later, and I am the founder and Chief Executive Officer of a thriving enterprise that has served Fortune 500 behemoths, government agencies, and mid-market companies in more than fifteen countries worldwide and in more than twenty states. Thanks to my idea and the support and encouragement of an extraordinary spouse, our business has expanded to the EGP Family of Companies (collectively "EGP", our family office portfolio of corporations). It is nothing short of a shining American success story, having its own real estate investment subsidiary, a private equity arm, and a distributorship business for a number of successful technology patents. I have been blessed to become a sought-after speaker and author. I get to travel to some of the most extraordinary places in the world. And on top of it all, I get to meet some really amazing people along the way. All of this is a lot of work, the degree and demands of which I never imagined. It has not been easy, but it absolutely has been worth it.

In what seems like an arduous journey but a relatively short amount of time, my daunting first step has led to giant steps. Because of those steps, my household has reaped dividends and experienced a fabulously rare journey—that is far from complete. I have worked for the universe and the universe has worked for me. I wanted to be more, and I became more. I took the first step.

PURPOSEFUL MILLIONAIRE POWER PLAY

1. Each person has within him or herself the power to make extraordinary decisions in life that will change the entire course of success. Some of these decisions are small, but some are overwhelming and gut-wrenching.

    You have made hard choices before that have benefited you, and you can do it again. Write three examples of when you came up with an idea and displayed extraordinary courage and power to change your circumstances. Close your eyes and reflect on how you manifested that courage and power and what it felt like. Then reflect on what remaining comfortable and NOT changing your status quo would have ultimately meant for your life. Resolve that this day forward you will always continue to manifest extraordinary courage in every decision that you make.

2. Repeat out loud five times, "I have everything that it takes to be healthy, wealthy, and happy. I am a Purposeful Millionaire."

CHAPTER THREE

GET OVER IT

TAKE A MOMENT to reflect on the tenor of the national presidential campaigns of 2016, or any national campaign in the past decade for that matter, to see what is really going on with our divisions. Access to money (and thus access to power) is the elephant in the room—it always has been. Folks, particularly politicians, skirt around talking about it because they, like me, were once taught that talking about money and power is impolite. Also, politicians do not talk about money and power because most of them have it, but many of their voters and constituents do not.

If you dig deeply enough, you will see that the undercurrent of pain in every social, racial, class-based, and political conversation concerns money, which leads to power, and ultimately to *respect*. Liberal, conservative, apolitical, black, white, brown, gay, straight, Jew, Muslim, Hindu, Christian, nonbeliever, Buddhist, rich, poor, man, woman, young, or old—whatever your identity is, I empathize with your disappointments and fears because fear never discriminates. It is the precursor to bitterness, and if left unchecked, can give birth to hatred. Hatred blocks all progress.

The tears of the demoralized black are just as salty as those of the disenfranchised white. They both want the same thing but do not understand that competition is not necessary, for the universe and its opportunities are infinite. She has enough for all of us to succeed. So dig deep within yourself, get over your self-limiting thoughts, stop worrying about what others are doing, and come up with an idea that will allow you to live purposefully and freely. You will receive the idea that will take your life to the next level by accepting the world for what it is—unpredictable, limitless, beautiful—and by rejecting fear, which includes letting go of your frustrations. Nobody ever promised us anything in this world, so we need to get over all of our fears and our complaints. Each of us has a responsibility to stop the complaining so we can achieve our dreams. We are so much better than our whining and finger-pointing, and the very act of complaining vacuums energy away from what we should be doing—working to achieve our goals.

As you come up with your idea to change your life or more closely examine what goal in your life you are currently working on, know that you must rid yourself of all fear and disappointment with the world for your idea to manifest into reality. This means letting go of all anger too.

Rule #3: It is okay to feel that the world of opportunity has left you behind, but get over it.

You should use any sadness, frustration, fear, and worry in your life to achieve something greater than yourself—to gain something—and to step out in faith. You must not dwell solely on what you have been taught or the feelings of limitation that take up residence in your mind. To step out in faith, you must first have faith in yourself. You have to renew your thoughts and train your mind. You have to know that what did *not* work in the past will not work in the future. You also have to know that even what *did* work in the past might not work in the future. You have to learn that your mind is your best friend. You have to understand that nothing in life—absolutely nothing—ever manifested itself without first originating in someone's mind. That mind can be yours. If anger, frustration, and fear are occupying space in your head, then they are also squeezing out space for opportunity and its gold. So get rid of those negative thoughts and fill your subconscious with positive, powerful, and affirming beliefs. Understand that when trained, disciplined, challenged, and maintained, the mind can make anything happen.

Every hour that you spend angry is an hour wasted.

—*Joyce Meyer*

When the anger is gone, great ideas are unleashed and come from all kinds of people with all kinds of circumstances. Such people draw on their innermost strength as well as the power of their belief system.

There are countless belief systems, and we might come from many different backgrounds and may not all call our God the same thing. But that's okay: we are all in this game of overcoming disappointment and fear together. My ethnicity at its raw genetically-tested essence is split right down the middle as half African and half European—and my religious, personal, and spiritual beliefs—based upon a Baptist upbringing and now a non-judgmental, non-denominational, unconditionally loving and caring spirituality (whose force I call the "universe")—may not be the same as yours, but we are in this race together. So let's stop the arguing and finger-pointing. Let's start focusing within.

> We may not know where our paths lead, but we know that they are being directed in the same way.
>
> —*Coach John Wooden*

To some extent, we are our own greatest obstacle. Focusing on the sunshine in our lives instead of the darkness will open our minds to lives of greater abundance and happiness. Continue reading to learn more about how you can make this happen.

Rule #4: Replace negative thoughts
with radically positive affirmations.

The thoughts that you harbor in the privacy of your mind, including frustration and fear hold infinite power. They have the ability to mutilate your creativity and idea-creating capabilities as well as any possible positive outcome that could ever possibly come from them. *Your thoughts matter more than you can imagine.* You must discard negative thoughts and work to make room for new thoughts and ideas. Emboldened by hard work, vision, drive, strategy, a bit of luck, and most of all, a positive attitude, the mind can create circumstances that innovate powerful ideas that create cash, the currency that makes the world go round. More than anything, you must understand that access to more dollars requires that a door be opened, starting with the door of your mind.

Just as every person breathing on this earth has an innate desire to be loved by someone, people have a yearning for money or a desire for the power and privilege associated with it, but a confusion about how to get it. For some, this confusion and frustration have caused a deep wound, or even a distrust of our government—the same government whose very Founding Fathers promised that all men, including you, are created equal. If you find this proclamation to be false or disturbing, get over it. Be brave and go out and create your own equality.

One way to replace negative thoughts with powerful positive thoughts is by repeating affirmations to yourself throughout your day. Such affirmations include *I have everything it takes to succeed in life. I am just as powerful as my thoughts,* and *only I can limit the strength that is within me.* These positive words do more than remind you of your inner power: they replace self-doubt with inner peace and self-confidence. They push out the negative and intrinsically pull in the positive. I believe that if everyone in the world repeated such positive affirmations to him or herself at least ten times during the day when self-doubt inevitably creeps in, this world would be a much better place. Make the world a better place right now, starting with you.

PURPOSEFUL MILLIONAIRE POWER PLAY

Repeat out loud five times, "I have everything that it takes to succeed in life. I am just as powerful as my thoughts. Only I can limit the power that is within me. I have everything that it takes to be healthy, wealthy, and happy. I am a Purposeful Millionaire."

CHAPTER FOUR

LEARN MORE, EARN MORE

DID YOU KNOW that the majority of people across the world will read fewer than five books cover-to-cover in their entire lifetime? How depressing. Some do not have access to books or education while many others who do have access say that they are too *busy* doing other things. I know some incredibly busy people with tremendous responsibilities who still find the time to read, so perhaps the non-readers were too *busy* watching TV, wasting time on social media, or gossiping. In spite of their accomplishments, many busy people still want more out of life. They are not satisfied–they read.

Satisfaction is the sofa upon which comfort and laziness sit. This book is obviously not for people who are satisfied, so share it only with people within your circle of influence who you are absolutely confident want to take their lives to the next level. This book is for hungry people from all walks of life who simply want more than what the world has offered them. Like folks who do not wish to find the time to read, you could be playing Pokémon right now, sitting on the sofa, or shooting the breeze over a six-pack of beer. But you are not–you are reading this guide. You most likely already know that simply reading the right material that nourishes your mind can make you feel better than any *happy pill* any doctor could offer. You are doing the work and receiving its automatic benefit.

This high road of educating yourself that you are traveling will heighten your consciousness, and you will be certain to get a great deal from the lessons and self-reflection required by being an active reader throughout your lifetime. The additional good news is that you are one of the select few who value the power of deeper knowledge, which can in turn become expertise, and thus be wonderfully lucrative! That is why you must master the understanding of the following rules about how knowledge can and will be your passport to greater achievement and financial success.

Rule #5: To earn more, you must learn more! Knowledge creates empires. There is no substitute for knowledge. A lot of people pretend to be experts, but they are not.

I wish I knew all there is to know about self-mastery and business, but I do not. I wish that I could tell you that I had an amazing mentor or role model who shepherded me through a smooth, blissfully high-stepping professional journey to success and that each day for me is like being a kid in a candy store. It is not. My journey has been filled with abrupt detours and personal "aha" moments. There was no uncle, no big brother, no sage father, no software app, no proprietary guidebook, and certainly no special mentor to show me the ropes. I acknowledge that there have been gracious folks along the way, and each one blessed me with love and encouragement, while others have helped to open doors for me. But there was no coach, no mentor, no holder of the magic key. I learned by trial and error. And, I learned by doing what Mark Cuban and other self-made billionaires call, "RTFM" (Read(ing) The Frickin' Manual).

I spent days and nights reading for hours (I still do and have never missed a day without picking up a book) about how to hone my personal and professional self; how to succeed in business and life; how to develop a startup; how to be a great family man; how to understand business marketplaces; how to expand a brand; how to be what I was not taught to be; how not to be a miseducated fool; how to be a respected leader; how to give my gifts of authenticity, love, and purposefulness to the world; how to advance internal business infrastructure, processes, and controls; and how to kick other people's derrieres in business. All of these skills were gained by experience as well as from reading books, just like this one. I applied the lessons found in them—which prepared me for a higher level of success. I read them, reread them, scribbled in them, dog-eared their pages, and hung Post-it notes with their most meaningful passages. Most importantly, I did more than just read them—I applied their teachings. I knew that knowledge without application is useless, so I made darn sure not to be reading in vain. I trust that you will do the same with this book.

Rule #6: Stop searching for someone to hand you the keys to success or to show you where they are. They are already in your hands. You just have to unlock the door of your mind.

Like me, my guess is that you have no aunt, uncle, or mentor to hold your hand through the everlasting journey to greatness. If you do, that's nice. You have a head start, so be grateful for that. But along the way most others will be approached not by a wise mentor but by people who lack substantial accomplishments who tell you that they know everything about the world and its strife merely because of the struggles that they have seen and claim to have survived. Don't listen to them. They are not mentors. They are naysayers. They are distractions who cast gloom with messages that are antithetical to a consciousness of abundance. Never take someone's advice who is not where you want to be in life. When I was a teenager, I had a much older family member tell me that I was a crazy for dreaming of leaving Lynchburg when I could easily get a good job at the local factory and make all the overtime money I wanted. Good thing I did not follow his advice!

Self-styled mentors will offer "wisdom" though they are still not willing to RTFM or pick up any book about how to achieve true success even if the book is handed to them for free. If you never find a great mentor, become your own mentor. Just stop waiting for someone special to show up and guide you, when you already have inner strength, self-discipline, and this book in your hand as a light to guide your life forward.

Rule #7: Differentiate yourself as
a true subject matter expert.

Fortunately for me, when I was a child, God came to me in the form of education and knowledge. Books were more than tools for expanding my knowledge base. They were and still are for me a spiritual form of grace, a religious experience, and a moment of recognition about the breathtaking vastness of the world and all that I could be in it. Books opened my eyes to possibility, and each one I read was a profound rejection of some of the circumstances in which I found myself in my parents' house, as well as the poverty consciousness that I had inherited. Books were liberty for me, and I basked in their warm, welcoming sunlight of freedom. Each glimpse at freedom led to new ideas about how the world worked; I found new opportunities and blessings, all of which would work in sync to build my future professional successes.

This application of knowledge found in books can work for anyone in any profession. It empowered me to become a *subject matter expert* on management consulting, executive coaching, corporate financial and operational strategy, and some other complex business affairs. People and corporate clients seek out me and my firm's expertise, and they pay us handsomely for our knowledge. The greater knowledge that you are accumulating will one day benefit you too. Not even a fool pays for ignorance. A wise person pays for expertise, often at whatever price the marketplace demands.

Very few people are willing to do the work that you are doing right now by reading this book and doing its exercises, so this will help you to *out-compete* them on your journey to success. Apply this book right now and others as your secret weapon for achieving your goals. I have received some guidance from special people in my life, but I never waited around on anyone else to bring myself to take action. Let other people talk about their goals and the special people or mentors that they believe they need in their lives to achieve them. While they are professing their ignorance, you should be busy reading, researching, accumulating knowledge, working on achieving your dream, and building your empire.

Not knowing can be the most dangerous place to be.

—*Unknown*

As you work on your dream, know that you will have questions along the way and that these strategies for success, and some of the keys to achieving everything that you want out of life, can be found in business, financial literacy, self-help books, websites, newspapers, magazines, and other periodicals that are focused on investments, entrepreneurialism, self-uplift, motivation, personal growth, opportunity, and expansion. They cannot be found on drunken reality TV or in Cosmo magazine.

To increase your wealth, you must simply study and apply the art and science of the acquisition of wealth, or at a bare minimum, devote time to listen to meaningful audio books and podcasts on a daily basis. Do not feel overwhelmed. Just read good literature and listen to the right things that are relevant and valuable to your journey, and because you are reading my manual for success, you already get what RTFM is all about. Fill your head with positive knowledge that will push you forward on your journey.

What I have read over the years has made light bulbs go off in my head and given me ideas that have made me money as well as brought me a sense of achievement. As such, my daily readings create a hunger for more knowledge, for new best practices, for more data, and for inspiration about how to be better in all that I do in life. Stay hungry for knowledge, and use that knowledge to hone your gift to the world. You will be certain to succeed. More than anything, you will have a much better understanding of the value of your knowledge and thus your time—something that you should scrupulously manage.

Rule #8: Always use your time wisely. It is an opportunity for you to apply your expertise. You are running out of time, and your life is much shorter than you think.

I am grateful for my blessings and cherish them to such an extent that I am determined to treat people right, to think big, to always take the high road when faced with difficult decisions, to execute my ideas and plans, and to not waste any of my remaining time left here on this earth. In so doing, I find no purpose in hanging out with people just to hang out. I find no need to watch TV unless it can be informational and thus help me to improve my business affairs, personal life, or leadership style. I spend very little time loafing because loafing is not fulfilling to me. Knowing that I might be getting behind stresses me out. And besides, I find working and reading to be absolutely delightful and somewhat soothing as I know that both are helping me to sharpen EGP's competitive edge. Once you identify the idea that will create your empire, I know that this will be the case for you too.

> The most important aspect of becoming a millionaire is the person you must become in order to accumulate a million dollars in the first place.
>
> *–Jim Rohn*

For me, these positive feelings of accomplishment come partially from the fact that I am getting ahead. To paraphrase Robert Kiyosaki, *the biggest difference between self-made wealthy people and poor people is what they do in their spare time!* So use your time wisely, step away from the TV. Read books that enlighten you on how to master your chances of success while you have the breath to do so. Our lives are short. I am quickly running out of time in this world, and you are too. Living four score and ten is certainly not guaranteed–my drowning accident reminds me of that every day. By becoming a great controller of your time, you will learn that it takes courage to say no to people and activities that waste your time and that the comfort that they achieve by being blissfully ignorant is highly overrated. Simply put, say "heck no" to any and everything that does not add value to your life or your financial affairs. Your sanity, consciousness, and bank account will all be glad that you did.

Rule #9: Always choose courage over comfort. Doing that takes an exceptional person. Exceptional people are different, and that is what makes them exceptional.

All this talk about learning more, becoming an expert at your craft, and mastering the use of your time can be pretty daunting. Doing so is far from easy and light years from the trappings of comfort and the abandonment of ambition. As you begin this new approach to learning more and thus being more, know that comfort is so very overrated. Though your old ways of doing things may have been comfortable for you, they were not the best or most efficient ways, and the marketplace did not reward you for it. Otherwise, you would not be reading this book.

When people are comfortable, they are not driven to improve or stretch themselves. They dwell in the predictability of their current circumstances, which does nothing more than hit the pause button on any journey whatsoever toward mastery of self, greater abundance, and happiness. Furthermore, many people are too lazy or so arrogant that they believe that their minds are capable of creating the rules of the game on their own before having achieved anything significant in their lives. You now know better than that. The game is much too complex to pull out of the sky one's own untested "how-to" guide, which is nothing more than a crapshoot at the game of success. That is why you must be courageous, get out there, forget about being comfortable, and follow the rules in this book.

Courage is the most important of all the virtues because without courage you cannot practice any other virtue consistently.

—*Maya Angelou*

Forget about the creature comforts of life and know that you are meant to experience comforts that will come to you at a level that you never imagined, once you are much farther along on your journey. That comfort may arrive in the form of personal satisfaction, peace of mind, or a sense of tremendous accomplishment. It also may come in the form of material luxuries if those are what you want. The courage that you are finding within yourself and the extra effort that you are putting in to getting more out of your life is not for naught. The marketplace does not reward dummies unless they get lucky and pick the right Powerball or Lotto numbers. The marketplace rewards masters who practice creativity, courage, and discipline consistently. With that understanding, you are doing the work to prepare for an epic life, the life of a Purposeful Millionaire. Don't doubt yourself. And most certainly, don't look back.

Keep pushing forward. Do the exercises and continue reading. You are well on your way.

PURPOSEFUL MILLIONAIRE POWER PLAY

1. How you live in this world is directly dictated by what you think about yourself. How you interpret challenges, setbacks, and criticism is your choice. To create a mindset of abundance and happiness, changing what you think about yourself and your circumstances is the first and most courageous step.

   a. Make a list of ten things, people, or problems that you believe are holding you back from accomplishing your dreams. (These problems may be personal, professional, or socio-political, or they may relate to specific people in your life. Just be specific about what exactly you believe is holding you back.)

   b. Say out loud, "I will no longer allow myself to hold me back AND I will no longer allow _____ (name the ten things from part a) to hold me back. I have everything it takes to succeed in life!" Repeat this list out loud to yourself five times daily.

2. Now repeat out loud five times, "I have everything that it takes to be healthy, wealthy, and happy. I am a Purposeful Millionaire."

CHAPTER FIVE

ASK WITH SPECIFICITY– THEN DO THE WORK!

When you say a prayer, move your feet.

—African proverb

MONEY IS SPIRITUAL. Everything about it is. It is a feeling. It is a force. It is among the highest of currencies. Its potential is created in one's mind and realized only when willpower and discipline meet opportunity. It is gained, lost, or misused all by the force of the mind of the one in whose hands it lies. It is more delicate than a newborn child. It should always be handled with care, caution, respect, and a tireless spirit to grow it.

With that said, the accumulation of money is neither mysterious nor complicated. People just seem to make it that way. One evening after finishing up a long day at the office, I invited an old college buddy to go to dinner with me. He had flown back to the States from a long stint living abroad and was eager to share the details of his new life with me. As we sat down to dinner, my friend looked at me and asked if he could ask me a personal question. He said, "So J-Now (my nickname), you appear to be happy, healthy, and wealthy, and you are a heck of a lot different from our old college classmates. I knew you were different back then, but it is so obvious that you are different now. Can you talk to me about how you did it? What's the magic recipe for all this?"

Needless to say, the question caught me off guard since we had spent most of our dinner together telling silly jokes and reminiscing about our college days. After thinking for a few seconds, I stated bluntly without reservation, "First, I asked for it." He looked at me as though I had two heads. Then I joked, "I wanted it, and I was willing to do the work and made some key sacrifices along the way, including spending less time partying with you in college!" He laughed. I became serious. "All of this has been achieved over time because of a series of very specific, non-generalized ideas that I was willing to take the first step on. Then one good decision led to another, which led to another, which led to small victories. I was able to make good decisions because I always put my subconscious first and focused on nourishing and enriching my mindset with positive thoughts. Some of my small victories turned into larger victories. And the cycle has repeated itself again and again. It was all that simple."

I explained to my friend my simple approach to achieving my dreams: living a structured life of daily disciplines, or, better yet, daily good habits, is ultimately key to both personal and professional success. The most important daily discipline is keeping my mind in the right place. This means always staying positive and being absolutely clear about my wishes and intentions while asking the universe with specificity for each blessing.

Little did I know at the time, a simple question posed by an old friend would become one of the geneses for *The Purposeful Millionaire*. I wanted to help out a friend with some advice so that he could reach a higher level of financial success and happiness in his life, and it made me think, "Why not share this gold with the rest of the world? Why not write a book? I want to see others do it too!" Hence, my mission soon became to share my success formula and fifty-two rules with as many people as possible.

I continued talking up some of my rituals, including doing meditation and yoga, spending ample time outdoors, and eating clean foods (limiting sugar and caffeine consumption, etc.), all of which I do on a daily basis to keep my mind clean, clear, and positive. My friend sighed and expounded on circumstances that had challenged him in his personal and professional journeys, but he became somewhat dismissive: "Bro, I get what you are talking about, but you sound like Mr. Perfect. Aren't you just trying to figure out this life thing just like everyone else? Adults are just like children—trying to figure out the world each day and how things work, and you talk as though you know all the answers."

His tone and body language (which included a neck roll or two) were showing signs of frustration, and he knew that it irritated me when people assume that they can call me "bro," so after taking a long deep breath and trying not to look at him sideways, I responded, "Look, not really. Instead of complaining, making excuses, or being jealous of others, I simply understand the rules of the game of advancement in life and the work that is required to achieve true happiness. If you opened your ears and listened, maybe you could learn the rules too and apply them to your life. I believe in mastery of myself, and I personally believe that James is the only thing that can limit James. I am willing to do the work and to execute my plans based upon those rules. I am not bragging. I was just trying to answer your question." Whew, I am normally a pretty calm dude, but he had gotten under my skin. I had said a mouthful.

That evening, once I was finally able to get my friend to step down from the pulpit of self-pity, I redirected the conversation toward self-reflection, abundance consciousness, and purposefulness. I bounced some questions off of him in an attempt to demystify his preconceived notions of how success is achieved: *What makes some people successful and others not? Why is it that someone who lacks a head start in life can get so much farther than one who has was born into tremendous advantages? What ultimately separates the victors from the meddlers in the journey of life? Why do so many people struggle to be happy, whether they are rich or poor? And more important than anything, how do success, wealth, and happiness interplay with each other?*

None of these questions could be fully answered in one evening. However, they would go on to serve as the foundation for our later conversations on demystifying success. As I recounted stories regarding my belief system as well as the work that I did to achieve my dreams, my friend listened closely. What follows is some of the groundwork we covered in that conversation and how it can help bring abundance to your life.

Rule #10: Spend the bulk of your time on executing your ideas, not on creating the perfect idea or on hashing out every imaginable detail of a plan.

Everyone has ideas. Ideas are cheap. They are a dime a dozen and are useless unless someone acts upon them by doing the work until they come to full fruition. People who spin their wheels and get stuck in the idea phase (spending the majority of their time there instead of a small fraction of it) rarely make it to the planning phase on the pathway to execution.

Lots of people have ideas that go absolutely nowhere. I refuse to be an ideas guy who cannot create opportunities for himself. That would be boring to me and, quite frankly, would make me feel pretty pathetic. Nobody respects the ideas guy. People respect the guy who has accomplished something that he can proudly stick his name on. Each of us can easily name colleagues, friends, or family members who are stuck in the idea phase. They get excited about thoughts of what they *can* achieve, yet they do not follow through. Ultimately, whether the cause of their inertia is a hurdle created within their minds (usually the case) or an actual impenetrable barrier to success that cannot be overcome, these people are the ones who get so much less out of life than what it has to offer. Let's refresh our memories on what the recipe for success looks like, something that those folks either don't know or do not wish to understand:

Idea + Plan + Execution (90 percent of your time) = Success

Or, in other words:

Inspiration + Preparation + Perspiration (90 percent of your time) = Elevation

The outcome of the formula also relies on one element outside of one's own work—asking the universe for your blessing with excruciating specificity is the key. Then you can do the work. By being specific, you are clarifying the idea in your mind and setting yourself up for a meaningful planning phase in order to move to the execution phase. General requests, such as "I want a million dollars," followed by little or no action and no belief in oneself or a higher power generally lead to nothing.

Late in the evening, after my friend and I had continued our conversation about the formula in greater detail, which was basically the much shortened dialogic version of this entire book, he asked me about my faith: "Well when you apply the formula, is it just you doing the work or do you just allow some higher power to take control?" I answered, "Heck no!" and walked him through how the overall system works. Through faith, good works, and living up to our God-given potential, I believe that we are achieving our highest calling by doing what we were sent here to accomplish. And through hard work, people's relationship with their God becomes even closer because they must rely on that spiritual force for strength through the challenging times that certainly come along the journey of accomplishing anything major. When people are lazy and do not live up to their highest and fullest potential, I believe that there is no greater insult to their Higher Power.

Knowing this, I shared with him that I root myself in something that is immeasurably bigger than I am—the universe and all its glory. Such an approach to achievement is fundamentally different from a "go-it-alone" approach, and thus, the journey is much easier and more satisfying. All of us can achieve this higher level of focus and satisfaction by tapping into something other than ourselves, and when that is done, accomplishments above and beyond our original goal subsequently multiply with less effort. This approach to my ideas, my goals, and my achievements puts arrogance on the shelf and allows my true character and talent to be fully unleashed and illuminated. As my friend and I had another round of delightful tapas and Cabernet at the table that evening, I explained the next rule to him.

Rule #11: Know that you are not in this game alone. You will certainly need other people, but more important, you will need to be able to call on your universe for strength throughout your journey.

I am no theologian, and this book is *not* a book about religion, but rather, in some part about one's spiritual connectivity with the universe. This means having an unbreakable nexus with something other than yourself to do the work to elevate yourself toward greater achievement and purposefulness. These actions all boil down to having a renewed faith in yourself—something that so many people lack or confuse with religion. For me, I recite the words of the *Prayer of Jabez* daily, which remind me that the faith that I have in myself is rooted in my Higher Power and that that Higher Power can encourage me with nudges, reminding me that the world is my oyster if I choose to get off of the sofa and open it.

I take the words of the *Prayer of Jabez* with me wherever I go. They partially lay the foundation for reminding me to be clear in my requests of the universe, to follow through by doing the work, and to be a responsible guardian of each blessing received. In essence, I not only ask for the blessing but also do the work, appreciate the blessing, maintain the blessing, and cherish it without fail by thanking the universe for it. The *Prayer of Jabez* reads:

> Now Jabez was more honorable than his brothers, and his mother called his name Jabez, saying "Because I bore him in pain." And Jabez called on the God of Israel saying, "Oh that You would bless me indeed, and enlarge my territory, that Your hand would be with me, and that You would keep me from evil, that I may not cause pain!"
>
> *–1 Chronicles 4:9*

Jabez, in his prayer to God, asks that he be blessed and that as he is blessed, he be kept from evil so as not to cause pain to others. He appreciates what he knows will come into his life, and he is also aware that blessings require one to be a responsible shepherd of them, carefully tending to them without fail. In short, Jabez asks for favor and abundance and vows to be a trustworthy custodian of such–he understands the gravity of responsibility.

The *Prayer of Jabez* is simply a few words that nourish my consciousness. Similar to it, one can find all kinds of equally effective supplications across many religions and philosophies including Judaism, Islam, and ancient proverbs. For my nonbeliever friends, they could choose to learn about the powerhouses of energy vortices working within their body and soul, including the Seven Sacred Chakras. If you do not know about the Seven Sacred Chakras, regardless of your faith, I encourage you to do some research online to learn more about yourself and the infinite power within that you can tap into. Whatever your belief or value system is that anchors you to this world, use it to supplement the boldness and strength that you must find within yourself to take your life to the next level and beyond. You will need to call on your faith's or philosophy's words during times of challenge, but above all, know that you alone are the primary gatekeeper of any and all future successes.

Outside of scripture and religious writing, we can see ancient tried and true references to working with the universe as a partner in taking action, such as in the old African proverb that I have prominently placed in a frame on a bookshelf in my home's library. "When you say a prayer, move your feet," or in other words, you cannot just ask the universe for something: you must also be doing the work (moving your feet) to take your game to the next level and beyond. By doing the work, the universe witnesses you in deliberate action and will respond to you with favor and abundance.

Ask for it, do the work, and follow through. And as you do the work, remember to stop complaining. No one, including me, ever said that any of this would be easy. I will be the first to tell you that my work allows little idle time and that my obligations are complex and substantial. However, the blessings and opportunities in my life are something that others may not ever come close to fathoming. I am fine with the gravity of my responsibilities, and I believe that my universe is okay with that too because a person endowed with extraordinary responsibility must be a person who exhibits extraordinary capability. For these reasons, on your journey to becoming a Purposeful Millionaire, it is critical to draw nearer to the divine force and energy fields in your life. By doing so, you will forge a partnership that is unstoppable.

As you forge this unstoppable partnership, never fail to ask the universe with exquisite specificity for victory and prosperity in whatever you choose as your idea and goal. In so doing, the energy forces of the universe line up to create a pathway to make that goal come true. By applying this two-step process—praying with specificity and working for that prayer—your life will eventually be marked by increase, not decrease, and an attitude of appreciation will inevitably bring you more abundance. This is not to oversimplify the other action items that you must do to achieve your dreams, including improving your skills and applying the rules of this book. However, it is to say that in order to get something, you must ask for it *and* work for it.

Ask with specificity, pray, do the work over and over again, and your dreams shall be achieved.

PURPOSEFUL MILLIONAIRE POWER PLAY

1. Decisions often have a snowball effect. Bad decisions lead to more bad decisions and thus worse circumstances. Good decisions often lead to more good decisions and thus better circumstances.

    a. Reflect upon a time when you made a bad decision and it led to another bad decision(s) and worse circumstances.

    b. Reflect upon a time when you made an excellent decision and it led to another excellent decision(s) and better circumstances.

    c. Reflect upon the attitude and mindset that you need to consistently make better decisions going forward and how those good decisions will have an impact on your life.

    d. Before making any major decisions going forward in your life, commit to pulling out a piece of paper and list the pros as well as the cons of the decision. If the pros outweigh the cons, then your decision is likely a good one. Go for it! If the cons outweigh the pros, then the decision is likely a bad one. Don't do it!

2. The formula for success is simple. Write down the formula and place it in a prominent place in your home or office. You can tape it to the mirror in your bathroom or to your laptop. Put it in a place where you will not overlook or ignore it. **Idea + Plan + Execution (90 percent of your time) = Success.** Reflect upon your dreams and how much time you have been spending in each phase of the success

formula. Be honest with yourself. Are you stuck in the idea phase or are you spinning the wheels of analysis paralysis in the plan phase? Are you an "ideas" person who simply cannot execute? What will you do to get unstuck to move on to the next phase? Be specific.

3. The universe is your partner. For you to receive anything, you must be willing to do your part for the universe to do its part. Write down three <u>SPECIFIC</u> things that are achievable that you are willing to commit to doing all of the work for and will ask the universe to bless you with within one year or less. Say out loud five times, "I commit to executing my plan every day to receive _____ (name the three things) within one year or less."

4. Write down your favorite inspirational verse that reminds you that the universe is always working in your favor. Place that verse in the most prominent place in your home or office. For me, the *Prayer of Jabez* as well as the African proverb referenced in this chapter are the screensaver and wallpaper that I alternate on my smartphone and other electronic devices. The many times throughout the day that I use my devices I am reminded of the power of the universe working in my favor. I am reminded that my territory is constantly being enlarged so long as I ask for blessings with specificity and complete the work. What is your verse or mantra?

5. Repeat out loud five times, "I have everything that it takes to be healthy, wealthy, and happy. I am a Purposeful Millionaire."

PART II
THE PLAN
IDEA + *PLAN* + EXECUTION = SUCCESS

CHAPTER SIX

LOOK IN THE MIRROR–THAT'S YOUR GREATEST COMPETITION

I have come to the frightening conclusion that I am the decisive element. It is my personal approach that creates the climate.

It is my daily mood that makes the weather.

I possess tremendous power to make life miserable or joyous. If we treat people as they are, we make them worse. If we treat people as they ought to be, we help them become what they are capable of becoming.

—Goethe

I AM GOING to make you a promise right now. My promise is that if you find the self-discipline to do the things outlined in this chapter, you will have a much happier and more productive life. Your happier and more productive life will stem from achieving a higher level of mindfulness, which is a fancy way of saying self-awareness, or how you interpret the world. The definition that psychologists use is that *mindfulness is a technique in which one focuses one's full attention only on the present, experiencing thoughts, feelings, and sensations but not judging them.*

A higher level of mindfulness is what is required for you to come up with a plan that works so that you can achieve your dreams. A plan that is devised from a person who is not mindful or who lacks self-awareness will ultimately not succeed in the long haul. What I share with you in this chapter will help you to solidify your plan so that you can arrive at the execution phase—the most important phase—of your success journey as prepared as possible.

Mindfulness is the key to achieving sustainable happiness. It is critical to your growth to understand that happiness is a state of mind that is completely attainable and that to a great extent, we control the input and the output of our minds. The success journey is meant to be enjoyed, and how you manage your levels of happiness along the way will feed your plan and, quite frankly, help you to get to your ultimate goal. Getting there simply takes believing in yourself and fostering the discipline to take hold of this reality of the mind. Now let's learn more about how all of this mindfulness stuff works. Let me begin with myself as an example.

Simply put, all that I ever wanted to be and ever will be was first created in my mind. Nothing ever materialized to me in life, including wealth, that did not begin in my mind. I sculpted my current station in life long ago and continue to build upon the foundation that was laid decades ago when I learned how simply to use my mind to be my greatest tool. My plan that I created in my mind and worked toward was very simple: 1) get the heck out of Lynchburg, 2) get all the education I could (both in and out of the classroom), and 3) use that education to make as much money as I desired. My plan was that simple, and I was able to succeed because of my mindfulness. I promise you that as you become more disciplined in your mindfulness and apply it to your plan, you will change your life for the better. You will live in the moment, not getting stuck looking backward or forward. Now, let's start with the biggest challenge to your success and greatness: you.

Rule #12: You are your own best friend or your own worst enemy. Do not be your own greatest saboteur. Be your greatest cheerleader and muse in spite of what the world may have told you.

Knowing that you, not the world, are your greatest competition is the first step in realizing your greatness. One thing I enjoy the most is mentoring disadvantaged youth to help change the way that they see the world. It saddens me that many of these talented youngsters truly believe that the world is implacably against them. Their environments have buried from them the clear and liberating fact that this world is full of extraordinary possibilities. By knowing no better at all, these young people have allowed their families and the streets to condition them to think in terms of the world being their enemy instead of their oyster shell.

Fortunately, after a few weeks of working with some youth, I can tell when they start to "get it." It's almost as if a lightbulb goes off in their head. They get excited about the world, and they start to feel the joy that comes from having a positive outlook on the world. They are no longer thinking in terms of survival but in terms of opportunity, possibility, and conquest. These "aha" moments are incredible to witness. Some of the most exceptional Americans have come from less than fortunate circumstances—even horrible circumstances. And usually it was not luck that changed their lives.

No. They used their minds as tools to change their lives and to change their world. They would accept nothing less than their best.

> *Impossible* is just a big word thrown around by small men who find it easier to live in the world they have been given than to explore the power they have to change it. Impossible is not a fact. Impossible is not a declaration. It's a dare. Impossible is potential. Impossible is temporary.
>
> —*Muhammad Ali*

In 2016, *Time* published an article about exceptional families that had overcome difficult circumstances to raise extraordinarily successful children. The article highlighted how the parents had conditioned the children's subconscious with positive thinking about the great possibilities of the world. They rooted their children with high expectations of the world that would lay the foundation for them to grow up to become pioneers in their respective industries. The article reiterated the one thing in common that determined success: *the mind*.

Now a highly accomplished adult, one of the children of these power families noted that the awareness of his parents' positive outlook on the possibilities of the world created an "extreme intolerance for underperformance within oneself." That man, Joel Gay, is one of the youngest black CEOs ever to lead a publicly traded company, Energy Recovery; and his sister, Roxane Gay, is a professor and highly respected award-winning author.

As rats scurried around the basement apartment bed in which his three young daughters slept, Gino Rodriguez would whisper in the ears of each child as she slumbered, "I can and I will." Doing this every night for twenty years, Rodriguez noted, "You talk to the subconscious. You don't talk to the conscious." As the girls slept, Rodriguez would give his daughters a pep talk and wake them each morning with a round of jumping jacks. Then he would require them to look in the mirror and say, "Today is going to be a great day. I can and I will." Rodriguez was doing more than just whispering good thoughts in his children's ears: he was changing the way they interpreted their futures. He knew well that by planting the seeds of deliberateness, optimism, and a flinty worth ethic, his children would go far.

Given the chance to create a subconscious rooted in forward thinking and great possibilities instead of negativity and impossibility, one of Rodriguez's daughters would become a Harvard graduate and partner in a private equity firm. Another daughter would become medical director of one of the top clinics in the nation. And another daughter, Gina Rodriguez, would become the winner of a Golden Globe Award for Best Actress.

Planning ahead is a function of class—the rich plan for future generations, while the poor can often plan only for Saturday night.

—*Gloria Steinem*

The Rodriguezes might not have had a financial head start on the world, but they did have a psychological one. In spite of less than desirable living conditions—a woman was murdered in front of their home—given the dynamics of their household, compounded by the unlimited power of the psyche, they were prepared to make meaningful and powerful contributions to the world, one child at a time. Mr. Rodriguez taught his daughters that they were in control. The world was theirs for the taking.

Rule #13: Realize that any way that you
see yourself has been self-created.

First, the barriers that you believe the universe has created to stand against you are not created by the universe: they are created by you, *yourself,* and no one else. Second, the problems that you have are more important to you than they are to anyone else on the planet. Absolutely no one cares as much as you do about your own problems, so you must work to manage them properly in your head. These facts may seem harsh, and you may think that I am brutally unsympathetic; however, the truth is that our minds control whether or not we place an omnipotent lock on our ability to overcome our circumstances.

In America, anything can be overcome. Absolutely anything. Just ask the Rodriguezes and the Gays. Our democracy may not be perfect, and certain aspects of it may be unequal and unfair; however, America is not limiting. She is a land of opportunity. Unless we are born into slavery or shackled to the ground by an oppressive or autocratic government, we are free. Master your mind and you will already be free.

No barriers of possibility exist in my mind. A new business associate of mine asked me one day, "Isn't your *color* an issue for you in your high-profile career?" Taken aback by the bluntness of his question as he continued to backtrack and babble along, I took a few deep breaths while counting to ten to get myself together before responding, or worse yet, snapping. What he was basically asking is to what extent I saw myself shackled by race. (He also asked me some really off-the-cuff questions about my thoughts on affirmative action.) I retorted, "My mind is the only thing that can limit me. The color of my skin has nothing to do with my success, so long as

I do not create false barriers within my mind that limit what I can achieve."

As the conversation continued, I realized that as a Caucasian man born into a well-to-do New York family, he could possibly have been envious of my self-made success and the genuine smile that I wear on my face each day. Or he could simply be curious, not ignorant. He might have fairly wondered why I had achieved more at a markedly younger age than he had in spite of the *color* of my skin and my not having been provided the advantages of life that he had enjoyed. However, by the end of our conversation, I had surmised that his questions were a result of his willful ignorance and lack of tact. He was not a friend but rather a "frenemy" who instead of wanting to learn more about me and my story, focused on a critique of race, something that I have never considered a limitation for myself.

It is not the critic who counts, not the man who points out how the strong man stumbled, or where the doer of deeds could have done better. The credit belongs to the man who is actually in the arena, whose face is marred by dust and sweat and blood, who strives valiantly, who errs and comes short again and again, who knows the great enthusiasms, the great devotions, and spends himself in a worthy cause, who at best knows achievement and who at the worst if he fails at least fails while daring greatly so that his place shall never be with those cold and timid souls who know neither victory nor defeat.

—*President Theodore Roosevelt*

No matter what I did to steer the conversation toward mindset and achievement, he kept returning to the issue of race. I realized that I needed this person's antagonistic energy out of my life, so I jettisoned him with the quickness of a lightning flash. He would never understand my story or respect the real nature of my success, so I figured why should I waste the time getting to know him better? I had myself to focus on. I would rather look in the mirror each day to consider my potential greatness than be bogged down by ridiculous questions and possibly envy, also known as bull caca. You may have encountered instances like this from people in your life: from family, so-called friends, business associates, or neighbors. If the people around you do not lift you up, find others who do.

When we talk about societal barriers, it is not to say that it is not challenging or sometimes impossible for inner-city youth (whose day-to day-priority might be the struggle to stay alive) to escape their circumstances, which include discrimination and social and economic structures that have given them no ladders to climb. It is to say that when we believe that the world basically works for our good, regardless of our situation, we attract the right circumstances to our lives so that opportunity and a path out of repressive circumstances can be created.

The universe works for your good when you do not see the world as a series of limitations or as a series of impossible hurdles to overcome. I have read about and personally witnessed people who have climbed out of the most dangerous of inner-city ghettos or depressed Appalachian hovels to achieve great success. With that knowledge, you and I can do anything if we put our minds to it. You can create your own luck.

Rule #14: Get your mind right,
and your life will follow.

Mindfulness is the offspring of the self-healing cultivation of subconscious that is required for you to get your life in check. Healthy mindfulness is being at one with yourself. It is the releasing of unhealthy ego and arrogance, and listening to the little voice inside of your head. You can actually train that voice in your head to think and act a certain way. One of the best ways to get your mind right is to be sincerely grateful for the blessings that you do have in your life. Focus on what you have and where you want to go, not on what you don't have. If you think in terms of lack, you will lack. If you think in terms of what you do not have, you will not be blessed with more.

Meditating on happiness and expansion of your life with gratitude for all of your blessings will attract more great things and opportunities to you, and it will help your mind to stay in a place of humility and positive reflection. Meditate on happiness and peace each day, and make a mental list of all the things for which you are grateful. I know that writing down all of the things for which I am grateful would take me hours, if not days, to complete: the list grows every day. If you find yourself feeling ungrateful, pull out a piece of paper and start to write down your awesome blessings. If you cannot think of any blessings start with these: being alive, having a roof over your head that does not leak, breathing clean air, and living in a home with a toilet that flushes. Your list should be so long that it is impossible for you to complete. If you cannot come up with some kind of list, then I advise you to come back to this book when you are in a better frame of mind. The book will be here waiting for you when you are ready.

Every time you praise something, every time you appreciate something, every time you feel good about something, you are telling the universe, "More of this please. More of this please."

—*Abraham Hicks*

Throughout your day, work on mastering your mindfulness. If doubt, fear, or vulnerability ever creep into your psyche, take a sixty-second break to do some deep breathing and reflect on love and appreciation of yourself, your family, and the opportunities with which you have been blessed. After you have taken that sixty-second break, do it again. Then do it again. Some people never do this, but the recipe for this kind of breathing looks like this:

Inhale deeply and envision cool blue, cleansing air filled with positive thoughts and self-love circulating through your body. Smile.

Hold for five seconds.

Exhale deeply and envision hot red air with all negative thoughts, doubts, or fear leaving your body.

Hold for five seconds.

Inhale deeply and envision cool blue, cleansing air filled with positive thoughts and self-love circulating through your body. Smile.

Hold for five seconds.

Exhale deeply and envision hot red air

*with all negative thoughts, doubts,
or fear leaving your body.*

*Repeat until your mood is positive and
your smile becomes more natural.*

Because most people do not possess the mindfulness that you will work on growing each day as a Purposeful Millionaire, they are as out of touch with the feelings and thoughts that run through their minds as can be. Indeed, some of the happiest people in the world are those who have the least, and some of the most miserable people have the most. I think you will find that those folks who are happy have a higher appreciation and gratitude for their blessings in life than those who are not. They also know how to stop and smell the roses—and breathe. Unhappy people always want more, and nothing is ever enough whether they are wealthy or not, they are servants to their poverty consciousness. They are always comparing themselves to others and are busy worrying about what tomorrow might or might not bring. They do not know how to pause, reflect, and give thanks for what they already have. If you ever feel yourself falling into the hatches of ungratefulness, do the breathing and meditation exercise above. Repeat and repeat. It will help to wash any negativity from your soul.

Wouldn't it be great to be both rich and happy? Many people have done it. Think about the purposefulness, drive, curiosity, and joy for life of Sir Richard Branson, Oprah Winfrey, and Elon Musk. They have achieved great success because they began with mindful, nimble plans and also stayed mindful throughout their journeys. They understood that their minds must be their sharpest tools, in constant need of honing, and that they can live lives of great abundance and happiness by mastering mindfulness. You can do it too by simply getting your mind right—no shrink required. The best part about all of this is that it's free, so you have no excuse.

Breathe. Meditate. Reflect. Think nothing but positive thoughts about yourself, your world, and your future. Hear no evil, say no evil, speak no evil. Repeat. Repeat. Repeat.

PURPOSEFUL MILLIONAIRE POWER PLAY

1. Taking the time out to love yourself and forgive yourself each day is one of the most empowering things that you can do. As human beings, we have made mistakes and will continue to make mistakes even as we grow stronger and wiser on our journeys. These mistakes are preparing us to live out our lives on a higher plane, and without mistakes, there would be no learning.

   Whenever you feel yourself becoming discouraged, take a self-love break by focusing on the moment and forgiving yourself. Breathing is the key to receiving new energy and to letting go of any self-inflicted pain. Take a sixty-second break to do some deep breathing and reflect on love and appreciation for yourself, your family, and the opportunities with which you have been blessed—not on the things that have gone wrong and certainly not on the things that you are lacking in your life. After you have taken that sixty-second break, do it again. Then do it again. Some people never do this, but remember that the recipe for this kind of breathing looks like this:

Inhale deeply and envision cool blue,
cleansing air filled with positive
thoughts and self-love circulating
through your body. Smile.

Hold for five seconds.

Exhale deeply and envision hot
red air with all negative thoughts,
doubts, or fear leaving your body.

Hold for five seconds.

Inhale deeply and envision cool blue,
cleansing air filled with positive
thoughts and self-love circulating
through your body. Smile.

Hold for five seconds.

Exhale deeply and envision hot
red air with all negative thoughts,
doubts, or fear leaving your body.

Repeat until your mood is positive and your smile
becomes more natural.

2. Training your brain to think positively about your-self creates inner peace and personal power. Walk into your bathroom and look at yourself in the mirror for ninety seconds. Make eye contact with yourself, and reflect upon your life's journey. What is your mind telling you about yourself? What are the voices in your head saying about you? Are the voices saying

words of self-doubt? Are you angry? Are you upset with yourself for not having achieved more in life? Are you disappointed with your circumstances? Are you proud of who you are? Are you happy? Are you arrogant and in denial?

Once you have had an opportunity to digest these thoughts, write them down on a piece of paper, date them, and stash them away in a private place. Each time you look at yourself in the mirror for the next seven days, spend sixty seconds looking into your eyes, saying out loud to yourself, "I have everything that it takes to be healthy, wealthy, and happy. I am a Purposeful Millionaire."

At the end of seven days reflect on how you feel about yourself and shred, cut, or burn the negative thoughts that you had written about yourself seven days ago. After the seven days have ended, whenever you look into a mirror anywhere, always repeat the words to yourself, "I have everything that it takes to be healthy, wealthy, and happy. I am a Purposeful Millionaire."

3. Repeat out loud five times, "I have everything that it takes to be healthy, wealthy, and happy. I am a Purposeful Millionaire."

CHAPTER SEVEN

IF YOU FAIL TO PLAN, YOU PLAN TO FAIL

I HAVE ALWAYS been different. I have learned to like that about me—to embrace my uniqueness in its fullness. That very confidence in my uniqueness has served as the foundation for fulfilling my dreams. In school, I was the kid who was kind to teachers, did his homework, made good grades, had no interest in bugging his parents for fad clothes, followed instructions, and had really good manners. I was polite to a fault and was curious about the universe, particularly the world beyond good 'ole Lynchburg. This is not to say that I was perfect because I was not. I was a kid and also a human being. But I was notably different from my peers whom I grew up with in my hometown. Today, to my benefit, that difference still holds true.

It was not until I reached adulthood that I fully embraced the totality of the fact that I am a one-of-a-kind individual with an equally unique and strategic thought process, which has served me well in my business and personal life. As I reflect on my journey from being horribly bullied as a child to fully living the life of my dreams, one thing I believe is that the very kids who tortured me because of my "yes ma'am, no sir" manners were not just taking anger out on me for being different; they were probably also secretly perturbed because they could intuit that I was on the pathway to achieving more than they would ever be able to. I made the grades, led the organizations, did the right things, and stayed out of trouble. They saw that, and they hated it.

My parents taught me how to work hard and to be a gentleman, even if this behavior was not always popular at school. I appreciate that they taught me such a work ethic and graciousness. But as a kid, my life was heading in a fundamentally different direction, and the bullies saw that in me. Little did I know at the time that their bullying would prepare me with a toughness and a commitment to fairness and justice that would serve me beautifully in the legal and business worlds. Back then, I knew that by keeping my nose in the books and by working hard, I would be freed from the limitations of small town life and that I would go very far. I would pray, "Dear Lord, please take me far, far away from here." Indeed, He took me far away, and I am grateful for that. I asked the universe to deliver me. I came up with a plan to get out. And it worked.

With a good plan, all of us can succeed and create wealth in our lives. For some folks, having $10,000 in the bank is perfectly enough cash to have a sense of security and accomplishment. That is fine and respectable. For other folks, the number might be $10 million or much, much more. Whatever the case, if you do not create a plan and stick to the daily discipline that is required to invest, create multiple sources of income, and avoid living beyond your means, then it's going to be pretty hard to achieve any significant financial success. Let's start with some rock-solid rules for your wealth plan.

Rule #15: Never underestimate the
power of freedom from debt.

As Americans, we tend to overspend and save much less than we should. For folks in the middle class and above, that trend can be reversed simply by spending less. I have had a credit card since my first year of college, but I have never carried a balance. I did not do this because I wanted to live a boring life and not reward myself with gifts and travel. I did this because I wanted freedom. I did not wish to be encumbered by debt because carrying debt is like carrying an eight-hundred-pound gorilla on my back everywhere I go.

Not having debt brings a little pep to my step. It makes me feel agile and unencumbered. I do not feel weighed down and I have access to options. As I have done throughout my journey, ask yourself these questions: could a smaller house be just as enjoyable as a larger house that requires more maintenance and TLC? Could a certified pre-owned standard car with an awesome warranty get you from point A to point B just as well as a brand new exotic car? Bigger things and more luxurious things cost more money than perfectly functional standard things (note: the oil change for a Ferrari can be more than $800 and the car requires thousands of dollars in annual maintenance). Such levels of care for luxury or exotic items requires more of your time. Believe me, I have plenty of stories to tell about that certain *why-in-the-gadzooks-did-I-buy-this-overpriced-high-maintenance-piece-of-junk.* Isn't time a form of currency just like money? But the good news is that I have learned my lesson—luxury items can be double whammies sucking up both money and time, so I do my best to simplify my life and surround my things that are comfortable, reliable, and as maintenance free as possible. Now that's freedom!

Your ability to decide your destiny is tainted by the amount you owe.

—*W.E.B. Du Bois*

We all waste money, including me, but regardless of our station in wealth we should strive to be less wasteful each day—this is just as good for the soul as it is for the environment. If you do not believe that you waste money, I encourage you to look in your junk drawers, closets, garage, or filing cabinets to remind yourself that we all fall short from time to time and buy things that we don't truly need. And a lot of the things that we buy are absolute junk. I admit that my recovering addiction to Amazon Prime has littered my closets with more useless gadgets than I would like to acknowledge. But I am working on fixing that. I am not perfect and am constantly working on ways to reduce unnecessary consumption.

The good news is that I have no credit card debt, and the trinkets are cheap to me. They have no impact whatsoever on my net worth or on the ability of my assets to generate income. If you are not in the same boat, I encourage you to do as I did in the beginning: buy less, reduce your debt, and live off of less. Having less debt, or better yet, no debt, will give you a sense of freedom and lightness that will put a big smile on your face.

The ability to simplify means to eliminate the unnecessary so that the necessary can speak.

—*Hans Hoffman*

By buying and spending less, you will find that your life is simplified and uncluttered, and you may gain a sense of liberation from not having your home packed with junk. This is not to say that you don't deserve or need certain material things; just take a very conscious approach to buying. A rule that changed my spending habits was to *focus on quality, not on quantity.* High-quality classic items are made well, last longer, and do not go out of style quickly. I have applied this rule to my dress shoe collection, which consists of four pairs of handmade very high-quality shoes made in London of the same brand and style. I love these wingtips. I've worn them and resoled them for several years now and get compliments on them all the time. They are simple, elegant, built to last, and I won't have to waste my time shoe shopping any time soon. I apply the same rule to shoes as I do to all liabilities, which are non-asset items in my life.

Liabilities or non-assets are among the things that are bought in stores or online. They do not generate income and never will—they suck up money. Liabilities lose money. Whenever you buy something, first ask yourself, "Is this is an asset or a liability?" If it is a liability, then ask yourself, "Do I really *need* this, or is it something that I just *want?*" If the item is something that you need, then ask yourself "Is it well-made, and will it not need replacing any time soon?" By asking these questions before each purchase, you will soon spend your money on buying necessities with an eye only on quality, not quantity. For me, this saves me money and limits clutter in my home. And to top it all off, we all look better wearing high-quality stuff! This practice also saves me precious time. Instead of shopping, I am reading, writing, working, researching, and investing in assets like real estate, stocks, and private equity funds (which continue to increase my *net* worth). Or I am traveling somewhere fabulous—and I still get to look good doing it (which increases my *self* worth).

Rule number one: never lose money. Rule number two: never forget rule number one.

—*Warren Buffett*

It may shock some folks to learn that I do not consider my homestead an asset; it generates no income for me and is a cash sink. Though the value of the property has increased significantly over the years, which creates additional market value (free money if I sell), the house and the grounds are collectively a luxury item, or a high-maintenance toy, which requires a high-priced staff to help me care for them. I cannot benefit financially from my homestead until I sell it. When I sell it, I will need another home, which is another liability, so now you get my gist.

Rule #16: Never count on your
home to create wealth for you.

The homestead is simply an example of one badass toy that I enjoy, and I put the proper resources in place to care for it. However, it is *just* a toy and not a tool to make money. I understand that and always keep that in perspective—no house-flipping for me. As you create your plan, understand that your house is a place to live and that it has little to do with your ultimate financial goals unless it is income producing and you rent it out for profit. The popular wisdom in this country is that you should buy as much house as you can afford and that real estate markets always go up. This popular wisdom has gotten a lot of folks in trouble. Just recall the mid-to-late 2000s and the housing crisis which precipitated the Great Recession. I have more than one friend who lost his home. Let's commit to not going back to those days!

Now you may say that I have just encouraged you to live in a smaller house and that I am a hypocrite for living in an estate home with a view to die for. However, the claim of hypocrisy is not true. My homestead is not expensive for me at all—it is substantially less expensive than what I could really afford; however, I simply do not live beyond my virtue of frugality. Think about this example. A billionaire who buys a 2.5-million-dollar Bugatti Chiron (a liability unless the car unexpectedly becomes a collector's item and turns into an asset) with cash is *not* overspending: so long as the income generated by his assets far exceeds the one-time cost of the liability, then he can buy whatever he pleases.

Understand that people are able to live at substantially different levels of purchasing power and financial freedom. Don't worry about what other people are doing. Be happy for them and focus on yourself. My life is simplified with the liability of a house that is—just like those wingtips—extremely well-made, beautiful, and far less than what I could afford. You won't find me moving simply because the housing financial markets or economy fluctuates. As the saying goes, a key to getting wealthy is "one house, one spouse." Choose both judiciously!

Rule #17: Always spend substantially less than what you make.

I believe in *stealth wealth*, not in *flash your cash*. There are millions of people who spend more money than they make, because they love to impress others. This is no way to create a happy life. In fact, spending more than one makes creates anxiety and misery. And by living paycheck to paycheck or by using credit cards to buy unnecessary things, folks eliminate opportunities to create wealth; and without money, any plan that they ever come up with is dead on arrival.

> Do not save what is left after spending; instead spend what is left after saving.
>
> —*Warren Buffett*

As a business leader who started a company during the Great Recession, I learned early on that I needed to be bringing in more money than I was spending. This is not easy, and that is the reason why the majority of businesses fail within the first couple of years. In the beginning at Excel Global Partners, even if I was bringing in just a few hundred dollars more each month than was required to run the business, those funds went right back into the business to develop infrastructure and to prepare the business for additional growth. Those few hundred bucks, over time, would lay the foundation for greater opportunity and be the seed money for creating an extraordinary business, which expanded into a multi-company enterprise.

> There is no dignity quite so impressive, and no independence quite so important, as living within [below] your means.
>
> —*Calvin Coolidge*

In your life, setting aside more than you make will do the same thing. I have applied this rule to my life, and though I am far from cheap (I tip generously to service workers who take good care of me and appreciate high-quality items), I cut my own hair, cook my own meals and eat at home as much as possible, and once a year I go shopping to buy high-quality clothes that do not go out of style. When flying commercial, I sometimes fly coach if I find a good deal, especially when I am on a short-haul flight and traveling for leisure. I still get from point A to point B as if I had paid for a first-class fare.

Over the years, I have met some wonderful people riding in the back section of the plane who are not unlike me. Having the luck to sit beside these awesome, like-minded, self-made folks, some of whom are incredibly financially successful and prudent, has produced conversations that have resulted in introductions as well as business opportunities.

Rule #18: Use your money as a tool to advance your peace of mind. The true power of money is not about having things. It is about spiritual well-being and having options.

Something else that always makes me smile (I will admit, laugh) is that flying on a friend's jet is a lot more fun for me than owning one and perhaps always will be, particularly as my financial assets continue to grow. The friend pays for the overhead, the fuel, the headaches, the crew, and the maintenance of that depreciating asset, and I just get to tag along, have fun, and provide a little business strategy advice for free over a glass of wine with him or her. Tagging aboard other folks' luxury vessels—yachts included— is how some deep relationships have formed for me over the years. The relationship is reciprocal. Friends invite me, and in turn, they get my companionship along with trusted business or other advice for free. I get a fun experience and access to their toys, which I have no interest in maintaining. This quid pro quo works perfectly on both sides.

I learned a great deal from two different older friends over the years, both of whom separately have assets well north of $100 million and who did the whole private jet thing briefly. Both friends still fly on commercial airlines (and will only charter a plane when absolutely necessary). Now if only the people who sat beside them on the commercial planes actually knew their net worth!

These friends taught me that all I need is the financial wherewithal and relationships to have access to luxury toys. They also taught me, and I have learned by experience, that the joy and excitement of owning a new fancy toy quickly goes away after the first couple of months–that's just how the brain works. With my access-instead-of-ownership approach, I do not need to own as many fancy toys, manage them, maintain them, and watch them depreciate. Because of that discipline and ability to adhere to my growth plan—and the social skills I have to develop meaningful relationships—I will never go to bed another night worried about money. That's true joy for me. That kind of peace is priceless.

Merely knowing that I have access to life's full bounty or the ability to travel any way I please is liberating for me. This represents a fully self-aware approach to living life to its fullest while enjoying the blessings of being free of debt. To do this, you just have to have the discipline to live not within your means but, rather, much lower than your means. Keep your mind and ego in a peaceful place and push yourself to live with less and to be more and do more with fewer headaches. Being unencumbered by debt means never having to worry about next week, next month, or next year financially. You will get to live in the essence of each moment and without anxiety regarding cash. Few people ever get to experience this. I want you to have that experience too for the rest of your life. The feeling is incredible.

> If you make a million dollars a year and spend a million dollars a year, then you are still broke.
>
> *—Unknown*

Fortunately for me—and I hope for you too—my ego is not attached to any particular material thing. My ego is attached to my contributions and the authentic self-expression that I give to the world. Being of a certain level of financial liberation allows me to focus on my gifts to the world. It creates an unencumbered state of existence that empowers me to keep my mind focused on my own personal leadership advancement and business expansion. It also allows me to be the best man that I can possibly be. The more I am the best man that I can be at all times, the more opportunities for future expansion are magnetized toward me. Great spiritual wellness attracts great opportunity. That's the beauty of success!

Rule #19: Envision your highest success.

Envisioning my highest success has always been important to my planning for the future. Near the end of each year, I light some candles, close the door to the room, lie across the floor, and take whatever time I need to meditate, reflect, and think about the things that I have accomplished that year, as well as where I would like the next year to take me.

After this period of reflection, I pull out a 3'x2' vision board that I buy at the dollar store. I paste on quotes, scriptures, pictures of things I want (including photos illustrating examples of exceptional health, well-being, and happiness), financial goals (mock account balance and spreadsheets), and the smiling faces of beloved members of my family. (They are all so awesome, and I love them to tears; they are part of what motivates me.) I then take the ideas that I have pasted on the vision board, open my laptop, and expound upon them in a Word document by parlaying them into one-month planning goals—to be achieved in succession over the next twelve months—for me and my businesses.

By breaking down my goals into bits and pieces, I find that they become more attainable, more tangible. Over the years, I have achieved nearly everything that I have placed on my vision boards. The visions turned into reality because I was doing the work and the universe was also working for me. On days that I am down and need an immediate pick-me-up, I will pull out vision boards from past years and reflect on the blessings that the universe has brought me.

It brings tears to my eyes to see that some of the things that I envisioned long ago have come to complete fruition or beyond what I ever dreamed. The vision board exercise is a magnificent tool and one of the secrets to my success. It helps to ground me and keep me focused. It also forces me to hold myself accountable.

If I get into a slump, all it takes is a glance across my office at my vision board to keep me pushing along in the right direction. If you choose to create a vision board for yourself, be selective about those with whom you share it. Share it only with those who are likely to encourage you and lift you higher. I have already begged you earlier in the book to jettison discouraging, negative people from your life. You can do it! Keep the vision board to yourself, or share it only with your motivators, not your detractors. Trust me: I once learned this lesson the hard way.

> If you go to work on your goals, your goals will go to work on you. If you go to work on your plan, your plan will go to work on you. Whatever good things we build end up building us.
>
> —*Jim Rohn*

By planning with something like a vision board or a detailed outline of your goals for the coming months or year, you are setting the universe in motion to rise up to meet you and your goals. If envisioning a year down the road is too difficult for you, then do a vision board for one month or six weeks. The main thing is to have something to look forward to and to keep marching toward it. If you do not plan properly, you will be stuck in the motions of mediocrity: going to work every day; living paycheck to paycheck or on payday loans; and feeling no sense of accomplishment, fulfillment, or vigor about your life's trajectory or achievements. Beneath the surface, your life will lack purpose and will certainly lack any of the natural highs that come along with being proud of achieving something great.

> To attract money, you must focus on wealth. It is impossible to bring more money into your life when you are noticing you do not have enough because that means you are thinking thoughts that you do not have enough.
>
> —*Rhonda Byrne*

When you are clear and consistent about your intentions and the direction that you want your life to go, good things happen. Oprah said it best: "Be clear about your intention, and the universe will rise up to meet you wherever you are." To this point, Oprah also said, "Be thankful for what you have; you'll end up having more. If you concentrate on what you don't have, you will never have enough." Rock on, Oprah. These words could not be more true!

Don't overthink this stuff. It's not that complicated, but doing the work to achieve it is. "Analysis paralysis" in the planning stage is enough to stifle any dream. Just come up with a simple plan—whatever you think will work for you so long as your life is moving in a forward direction and your bank and investment accounts are increasing. This is not to say that every plan will always work out as you had wished because not all plans do. Just remain in unity with the universe, and stay flexible. Some people are so married to a plan that they ignore the universe's calling for them and end up throwing their lives away chasing the wrong plan. Don't be like them. Be open-minded and willing to make some changes along the way.

In addition, some folks waste their time asking other people what they believe is the universe's calling for them. Don't waste time like them. The biggest mistake you can make is to ask other people what you should do with your life. Trust me: I spent a year in medical school and three years in law school only to learn that I did not want to practice medicine or law! Just know that only some of my plans have worked out, but I keep picking myself up and moving forward. I make adjustments along the way so that I can listen to what the universe wants for me. I then step out on courage, time and again, knowing that the wonderful lightning of opportunity will never strike me if I am not willing to stand out in the rain.

Sometimes forces beyond your control will slam one door in your face only to open another door that leads to greater opportunity. This has happened to me time and again, but I go back to my plan, recalibrate, make a few alterations, and move on with my life with full vigor. Even when something unexpected or unfortunate happens to me, how I respond to it determines how long I will be miserable in that situation. I cannot control the universe, but I can control my reactions. We are all partners with the universe: we must do our part for the universe to do its part. The burden is not on the universe; the burden is on me to tap into the greatness of the universe. Knowing that, I control the choices I make, committing myself always to make good choices based upon my collective life experience and value system, and those choices inevitably determine my destination as well as my peace and happiness on the journey of life. With this mindset, I have learned that opportunity opens up for me in ways that are sometimes beyond belief. I have chosen to live *for a purpose on purpose*. The purpose was provided to me by the universe. I did not force someone else's calling into my life. I received the universe's calling for me, and my mission became pure joy.

The two most important days in your life are the day you were born, and the day you find out why.

–*Mark Twain*

With planning and hard, joy-filled work, anything is possible. Instead of working counter to the universe, magnetized by its energy and miraculous ways, I am working with it. The universe conspires to advance me, lift me up, and increase me all because I choose to live out my authentic mission and calling. Simply put, my mission is to live a life of pure authenticity and unflinching courage to help other people identify their mission and become their greatest, best selves. And, of course, one's greatest, best self is one who is not broke!

The mission comes to fruition because I am true to my calling and my mind stays wrapped in thoughts of my mission and in thoughts of abundance. Join me in doing the same.

Rule #20: If you are not willing to
do the work, nothing will work.

Maya Angelou once said something along the lines of Rule #20, and it is so very true. If you are like most folks, including myself, you will not get some kind of magical daily motivation to plow through your plan or get your work done. However, what you can do is set in place the daily disciplines and work ethic to ensure that you are constantly chipping away at your plan. This, of course, is called self-discipline.

What separates great achievers from those who only dream is self-discipline. No one ever cranked out a bestseller in twenty-four hours or became a multimillionaire overnight—unless he or she won the lottery or inherited the money. Money that comes quickly also leaves quickly, so just do the work.

A friend of mine who started with very little built his company over three decades of hard work. He earned several hundred million dollars from the sale of his global business and frequently jokes, "I am just a thirty-year overnight success story." He is one of the most humble men I know. His story is similar to the stories of so many other folks who just kept thinking positively and moving forward with their plans. Today, people call him for advice left and right, though thirty years ago people called him a workaholic.

The average call me obsessed; the successful call me for advice.

—*Grant Cardone*

Just keep chipping away at your plans and separate yourself from the folks who are always dreaming. Place yourself among the folks who are always executing. We only get one thousand four hundred and forty minutes in a day, and I am convinced that the vast majority of those folks, in business or not, spend a good deal of that time talking about their ideas and blowing smoke. So as you execute your plan, don't get discouraged. Things will not always go your way. Again, share your plans only with those who are likely to encourage you or provide constructive criticism and uplifting words. Know that your plan is just the starting point; self-discipline is what will get the plan across the bridge.

Like you, I certainly cannot see the future, but I can create a plan and chip away at it on a daily basis. The best way that I can create luck and predict the future is to keep myself disciplined in doing the work each day—all of it, even the tasks that I do not enjoy doing. The epigraph to this book is a quotation from a man who is one of the Western world's most famous artists whose artwork includes sculpture: "One can have no smaller or greater mastery than mastery of oneself." I like to think that Leonardo da Vinci thought of our ability to sculpt ourselves and our plans as a kind of self-mastery and self-discipline too. Compounded over time, my self-discipline has blessed me abundantly and allowed me to sculpt my future. Even when friends were disappointed because I could not make time to hang out with them or go to their birthday parties, I believe that my accomplishments have validated the choices I have made. That's a really good feeling. And now my friends tell me how much they like to brag about me because of my accomplishments. That's a really good feeling too. Everything always works out.

> The distance between your dreams and reality is
> called discipline.
>
> —*Unknown*

With a planned, balanced approach to finances (it ain't impossible y'all: just spend less than you make, invest wisely, don't follow fools' advice—because there are a lot of fools out there— plan out your dreams, envision success, and apply some radical self-discipline), you will become the captain of your future. You will be constantly building, constantly increasing, rarely decreasing. Remember that all of this positive action takes planning, so if you fail to plan, you most certainly will plan to fail. I am confident that by following these rules, each Purposeful Millionaire reading this book will become a planner, backed by the self-discipline to execute. The execution will bring accomplishment. Accomplishment will bring success.

PURPOSEFUL MILLIONAIRE POWER PLAY

1. To earn more money, you must spend less than you make. Too often people focus on increasing income, with little or no regard for their spending habits or propensity to waste. Take a few minutes to walk through your home to appreciate all of the nice things that you have accumulated. Now go to the part of your home where you store all of the unused items or junk that you have wasted money on. Indeed, every home has a junk drawer, a packed closet, or a garage that has lots of stuff stashed away, most of which are the result of wasted money. When you look at all of the unnecessary items, know that

---

they are all liabilities, not assets. They are not appreciating in value, and most of the junk has very little or no value. Reflect upon how it makes you feel to have spent your hard-earned money on these forgotten stowed items instead of investing in assets to increase your net worth. Are there other junk drawers in your life? Are you living up to Buffett's rule: "Never lose money"?

2. Now that you have had a moment to think about money that you have wasted on liabilities instead of assets, fill in the lines below:

    a. To become wealthier, I will spend less money on these things (liabilities):

        i.   _____

        ii. _____

        iii. _____

    b. b. To become wealthier, I will put aside more money for these things (assets):

        i.   _____

        ii. _____

        iii. _____

3. For wealth to be achieved, you must train your brain to think of yourself as already wealthy. People who are wealthy and wise do not think solely in terms of accumulation of fancy toys (which are liabilities); they think in terms of an accumulation of assets, which will make them even wealthier. If you are unsatisfied by the material possessions that you currently have, you will never have enough. When you think about

things that you want, tell yourself, "I *already* have those Gucci loafers or Christian Louboutin heels, so I don't need to waste my money on another pair." The point is to quiet the voice whispering in your head that says you *need* those new things to be happy. Happiness has no price tag.

4. Repeat out loud five times, "I have everything that it takes to be healthy, wealthy, and happy. I am a Purposeful Millionaire."

MULTIMILLIONAIRE POWER PLAY!

You will need at least one hour for this exercise, along with a quiet room, scissors, glue, a stack of old magazines, markers, a picture of yourself, and a poster board (you can find them at any craft or dollar store).

1. Start this exercise by doing a five-minute meditation. Breathe deeply and envision your greatest self. See yourself as fully fulfilled, healthy, and wealthy. Envision the people, places, and things that are all components of your ideal life. See yourself at your absolute best.

2. After the meditation, turn on some motivational music and flip through magazines to find pictures that represent your ideal life. These pictures may include people smiling, exotic locations, designer clothing, investment portfolios, luxury cars, homes, and so on. Cut the pictures out that best represent what you would like to have and paste them on the board. (Dream big, but don't forget about the earlier

lessons in the chapter about smart asset buying and frugality!)

3. Reflect on the quotes that have the most meaning to you—the ones that really empower you—and write them or paste them on your poster board.

4. Paste your picture on the board, and beside it, write out your personal mantra or the Purposeful Millionaire mantra, "I have everything that it takes to be healthy, wealthy, and happy. I am a Purposeful Millionaire."

5. Add any other photos, quotes, etc. to your vision board that will help you to remain inspired for the next 365 days. Be sure to write the start and end date on your board.

6. Place your board in a prominent place, or hang it on a wall; be sure to put the board in a conspicuous place that you see daily. Each day for the next year, look at your vision board and continue to work on retraining your mind for healthy self-esteem and success. Repeat this exercise annually as you continue to work toward your goals. Be sure to save your old vision boards because as you achieve your dreams over the years, you will be able to reflect upon how your plan came true—the blessings that the universe brought you because of the power of visualization, focus, and hard work!

CHAPTER EIGHT

YOU WILL BECOME PRECISELY WHAT YOU PLAN OR DON'T PLAN TO BE

I AM LUCKY to have a large network of friends who are not only successful but also good, kind, honest, and hard-working people. Three of my friends happen to be young dentists who practice in different parts of the country. Each one planned his respective idea for success in life and has a vastly different approach to life and business. Each dentist is doing exactly what he dreamed and precisely what he believes works best for himself in his dental practice and family life. Indeed, I consider each one a very happy man, and I enjoy spending time with all of them. They are living testimonials of the power of planning and following through on their plans by executing fully.

I believe that each one considers some aspect of the practice of dentistry his calling. However, because my three friends have such different goals, outlooks, and approaches to business, mentioning more about them will allow us to understand the diverse ways in which planning functions as a tool, as a roadmap for the mind to achieve whatever one wants out of life.

Rule #21: Not everyone has the same
dream, so tend to your own dream, and let
other people live out their dreams. Focus
on your plan and your plan only, and you
will achieve exactly what you desire.

Dentist Alex is a highly accomplished professional and a community pillar. He is well-known and universally liked across his community and is respected for his generosity and genial demeanor. His staff members love him, and he spends countless hours developing each of them to run the best dental practice in his town. His office is a well-run machine. Having graduated at the top of his dental school class, he possesses qualifications and certifications as a subject matter expert and is called upon by other dentists and oral surgeons to provide consulting on the most complex challenges. Part of Alex's plan was not only to be a great dentist, but to be a respected community member—and that he ably achieved. In Alex's town, there is not a candidate running for office that does not visit him because of his community and political influence. He is admired, connected, and powerful.

Alex has thrived. His solo practice generates a very comfortable living for him and his family. His practice consumes a great deal of his time. He is the hardest-working of workers and never seems to have a minute's rest. Nonetheless, the smile on his face is genuine, and he receives a great deal of satisfaction from his work. He is purpose-driven. He has achieved the American Dream, has a fantastic life partner and two kids, along with a lovely home in an upscale neighborhood and two luxury SUVs. Alex does not mind the toil that comes along with achieving his dream. In dental school, Alex made a plan to: 1) relocate to a midsize city in the Sun

Belt where he could enjoy warmer weather and a higher quality of life, 2) become a respected subject matter expert among dentists in his region, and 3) use the respect and connectedness to political power that he has earned as a tool to uplift his community. Alex achieved his plan and became exactly what he wanted to be. He is a very happy man.

❦

Dentist Bart graduated near the middle of his class from dental school and always enjoyed his job. He is a naturally smart person with enough people skills to keep his dental practice running smoothly. Bart's father was an entrepreneur who became a small businessman, so growing up, Bart was able to witness his father's struggles to grow the family business. Bart's father would often talk at the dinner table about having the capacity to own a couple more stores around town to scale the family business, increase revenue and his customer base, and thus increase profitability. Years later, in his very own dental practice, Bart would do the same thing.

Bart launched a small chain of dental clinics in his town. They are nice clinics and offer good dental care in a relaxed atmosphere. Bart enjoys the core business side of things and the internal business infrastructure that he has created. He leads three offices that are staffed with two other dentists, one office manager at each location, and a team of hygienists and other professionals.

All in all, Bart worked hard for a few years so that he could build his practice, and he now reaps the benefits of having done so. Bart has two homes, one in Colorado where he and his wife always vacation for at least two weeks in the winter for skiing and a comfortable estate home in his hometown in California. He has all the trappings of success including a twenty-four-foot ski boat, a sports car, and two luxury cars. Bart's workweek is usually less than forty hours, and he spends his free time volunteering for charitable causes, which helps both with business development and with providing financially disadvantaged patients a means of transportation to his dental practice.

Life is very good for Bart, and he has a fair amount of free time to explore whatever suits his fancy. In dental school, Bart's specific plan was to: 1) return to his hometown and marry his college sweetheart, 2) start one dental practice and use the earnings from it to open a second location and then another, and 3) have his business so well run that he could afford to own multiple homes and give significant amounts of time and resources to charitable causes by volunteering. Bart achieved his plan and became exactly what he wanted to be. He is a very happy man.

Dentist Chris was born into a family of success. His dad had invented a successful patent and later went on to scale an import-export company to a multimillion-dollar enterprise. From day one, Chris saw dental school as simply a means to an end. He was never in love with the practice, but he was in love with aspiring to be a bigtime businessman like his dad. He saw his dental practice as a vehicle for creating the life that he aspired to have, all fueled by the many lessons that his father had taught him as a child about the nuances of business, the power of compounding dollars, and the privileges that come along with owning a large-scale enterprise.

Chris's father wisely warned him that he would not inherit one cent from him upon his death, so he had better take his business teachings to heart and apply them to his life. Chris did just that. As a young dentist, Chris took out a small bank loan to start his own practice and then, once he got the business more established, he immediately took out another loan to expand the practice to one additional location. These were bank loans that were collateralized against his house, and Chris knew that if he defaulted, his home would be seized. Chris knew that the terms of the loans were daunting, so he busted his keister to pay them off and handled each dollar conservatively.

Chris worked hard enough to start his dental practice but worked even harder on a business plan to strategically expand his practice. Another like-minded dentist friend of his bought into his practice and also his business plan. The business partner was strong in areas where Chris was weak–because of that, Chris knew that the business plan would be a tremendous success. Each year, Chris and his business partner would commit to the ambitious and exhausting plan of opening three new locations and to hiring the best talent to run them, while they kept their hands on the levers of the business. They focused on strategic planning, infrastructure, processes and controls, accounting and financial system optimization, and exit strategy while developing strong relationships with several banks and lending institutions.

In addition, Chris and his business partner hired top interior designers and decked out each dental office in lush furniture and state-of-the art technology. They knew that getting people's minds off of the agony of being at the dentist's office would be key to developing their customer base. They were right. Though their clinics have a good reputation for the skills of their dentists, they are better known for their swanky interiors and the ability of their staff to make patients feel ensconced in luxury, and thus pampered and relaxed. Chris scaled the business based upon this concept. Today Chris is the majority owner of forty dental clinics across three states. Chris is a multimillionaire who enjoys vacationing at his fine homes in Hawaii as well as Sag Harbor–he has all the trappings of an extraordinary lifestyle.

Though Chris dabbles in the practice from time to time to keep his licensing and credentials up to date, he uses the majority of his time to review profit and loss statements and balance sheets, and in full disclosure, he has become a client of my firm. In dental school, Chris's specific plan was to: 1) use his degree to qualify him to get into the business of dentistry and find a good-fit business partner so that he could pursue his true passion—business; 2) borrow cash as soon as his first practice was profitable in order to open another practice and then another; and 3) put the majority of his business's earnings back into expanding the enterprise, which included improving the infrastructure of his business, launching new locations, and creating a franchise. Chris too is a very happy man. He achieved his plan and became exactly what he wanted to be.

Rule #22: Whatever you create in your mind and stick to, however great or small, you will achieve.

Though Alex, Bart, and Chris are three different people, each is successful in his own right. Each one has mastered a certain craft and each one has created jobs. Their respective journeys represent the challenges and blessings wrought by hard-working people who believe in themselves and their very specific American dreams. Important to note is that the only major difference in the outcome of their business dreams is scale. Chris has the largest enterprise, but to this day neither Alex nor Bart wishes to deal with something of such a magnitude. They are both delighted with what they have achieved and do not waste time comparing themselves to others. By coming up with his own respective idea, creating the plan, and executing it, each dentist has illustriously received from the universe exactly what he wanted from it.

Also, it is important to note that not one of the three inherited a practice from a parent or stepped into his business by being handed the opportunity. Over a beer or glass of wine, each one is always willing to share freely with me examples of the challenges that he has had to overcome as well as his absolute belief in the tool that he used to achieve his goals: the mind. The road was not easy for any of them, but the rewards have been precisely what they planned for and expected.

In the case of Alex, who is a great family man and respected community leader of formidable clout, his practice is most important to him. He is a popular and highly respected man of great integrity. Having created an upper-middle-class lifestyle for himself and his family, he is living his dream to the fullest. He envisioned his practice while in high school, worked toward that vision, and achieved it.

In the case of Bart, he is the first in his family ever to go to college and certainly the first in his family to climb successfully well above the middle-class line. Bart has created a work hard-play hard lifestyle, and he has a lot of fun enjoying the blessings that he has achieved. His business is large enough that he can write checks for charitable and philanthropic causes in which he believes. He also loves the fact that he can volunteer as much as he wishes for the same causes. He has been an emcee at several charity galas and is involved in arts philanthropy.

Bart envisioned a practice that would create for him the life that he wanted. He saw his practice as a tool to get to that lifestyle, and today he reaps the fruits of his labors. Growing up watching his dad and attending college business courses, Bart learned of the power of scaling business. The seed of successful entrepreneurialism was planted in his mind: he created a plan, worked toward that goal, and achieved it.

As for Chris, what can I say? For lack of better words, he is a baller. Chris had the advantage of being involved in and learning about business his entire life. That upbringing taught him some basics about business as well as the power of using bank money to grow a business. While growing up, Chris saw his father work and scale his corporation, and he knew that he possessed the toolkit (a good mind and the discipline to train it) to create something unique. When I talk with Chris, he always says, "Go big, or go home!" That is the philosophy by which he lives, and it has reaped dividends for him. Along his journey, Chris has not been averse to risk and has certainly not been free of hurdles to be overcome. He suffered a very public divorce several years ago, which was a hot mess, but he bounced back beautifully. He knows how to keep his mind in the right place, even during the worst of circumstances.

Chris knew that he was not in love with the practice of dentistry. He saw it as a means to an end, and he was willing to do the work to put his business and creative brain to use to create achievement. With more than four hundred employees and many different offices and homes, Chris enjoys the freedom and luxury that he has earned. He manages his stress levels by traveling in style on his newly-remodeled Bombardier Learjet 45 to wherever he dreams of going, which I have enjoyed traveling in as well.

Rule #23: For anything to be manifested in reality, it must first manifest itself in the mind.

The picture of what you want out of life must be so clear that when you dream, the dream is the same again and again so that you cannot tell the difference between being in reality and being in the dream. You must be able to taste, feel, smell, and hear the dream being manifested in all its glory. When you commit to a dream and do not change course because the dream is too slow coming to fruition or because achievement is "too hard," then your dream is destined to come true.

The timing for your blessing is ultimately up to the universe, but one thing is certain: if you do not first plan for it and do the work, it will never be achieved. Do this for all things in your life: good health, abundant living, wealth, and harmonious interpersonal and family relationships. Then watch what happens. You will not be disappointed.

PURPOSEFUL MILLIONAIRE POWER PLAY

1. To compare ourselves to others is human nature, but it is not constructive. Obsessively comparing oneself to others can be one of the most debilitating and dangerous habits imaginable. Just like Alex, Bart, and Chris, you must live your own dreams for yourself and stick to them to fulfill your true destiny. Take five minutes to reflect upon three people to whom you sometimes compare yourself. How does this exercise make you feel? How do they make you feel? Can you have a genuine relationship with these people? Now write down their names and fill in the lines:

   a. _____ (insert name) makes me feel green with envy because

_____ (write the reason why you are jealous of that person).

b. I will no longer limit my life or reduce my potential by comparing myself to or being envious of _____ (insert name) because I already have everything that it takes to be healthy, wealthy, and happy. I am a Purposeful Millionaire.

2. Write a short paragraph explaining why setting your own course in life, coming up with your own ideas and plans, and following your own dreams are important to you. Be very specific.

3. Write a letter to the person who makes you feel the most envious or inadequate. Explain why that person makes you feel this way and exactly what you will do in your life to no longer feel that envy. Once you have completed the letter and reflected upon it, lock it away in your private files or destroy it.

4. Repeat out loud five times, "I have everything that it takes to be healthy, wealthy, and happy. I am a Purposeful Millionaire."

CHAPTER NINE

EXPANSION REQUIRES CAPACITY

THE UNIVERSE WILL only ever give you what you have demonstrated the capacity to handle properly, so if your plan is not coming to fruition, do not be surprised. A good illustration of this can be found in a good friend of mine who is an entrepreneur that built her business from scratch some fifteen years ago. Her business, started as a sole proprietorship, has over the course of a little more than a decade grown to employing more than two hundred people. Because of her business's success, she lives in absolute financial abundance—a big house, luxury cars, a ranch, fine jewelry, fine artwork that adorns her homes, charity ball sponsorships, and frequent first-class travel all over the world.

Sheryl is what most observers would call a badass. I am so proud of her and all that she has accomplished—on her own. She puts on big girl pants every day, works hard, and runs nothing short of an empire. However, a couple of years ago she shared with me that her business had plateaued and that her net worth had remained relatively stagnant. In addition, she said that she was completely unhappy and felt little sense of accomplishment or satisfaction with life. When she told me this, I thought, "Say what?"

Looking from the outside in, one would wonder why her business profits had remained the same over the past few years since she had the experience of being a gritty entrepreneur who had bootstrapped her way to success a decade and a half ago. Why was her business not growing? Because I know her well, the answer was clear to me but not to her. The answer was that she had become her own worst enemy and is completely out of touch with herself and her blessings. Though she was doing the work, she was not in sync with the universe. Her negative attitude about her business and utter lack of appreciation for the blessings that she had received had become the greatest limiters to her success. Allow me to explain.

Rule #24: Always have an attitude of gratitude. It is a magnet for future blessings.

One day while discussing life, liberty, and other pursuits, Sheryl belted out to me, "I just get tired of taking care of all this crap! It consumes me. These houses, these cars, these social events are all so overwhelming. James, I am so exhausted." As we sat by her pool, she continued to pout, "Maybe I should move out of this giant house. I could buy a cute little car to get me from point A to point B and a one-bedroom condo. I would have so much less to take care of, and that would be so nice! Maybe I am just a failure. I cannot even get my business to grow. I am so ready to throw in the towel."

Sheryl appeared to be contradicting herself. In one breath she was suggesting that having less would make her life easier, while in the next breath she was crying about her not being able to grow her business. I had to intervene, so I responded, "Sheryl, just look at what you have already achieved, and show some gratitude! Years ago you showed the universe your capacity to handle your blessings while creating your empire, but now you are complaining and asking the world for less. That is precisely why your business has plateaued and why you are so unhappy." I expected Sheryl, who was known for her feistiness, to go postal on me at any moment. She did not.

I paused, looking her directly in the eye, and proclaimed, "Let me keep it real with you, Sheryl. Aren't you the same person who started with little more than a pile of student debt and discouragement from some of your friends and family fifteen years ago only to create a mini empire for yourself? You are constantly pouting, my friend, and I miss the old you." Whew—things were getting tense now. She responded to my first point, "Your comments are not true, James. I still work very hard, but this is just too much for me to take care of, and it is too much responsibility. And my business is not growing. All this stuff is a cash sieve." I retorted, "Well first change your attitude. Then get some gratitude, run your business better, and hire more good people to help you!"

Rule #25: Demonstrate the capacity to exquisitely care for your current blessings so that the universe will prepare more for you.

Sheryl paused for what seemed like a minute of silence. Tears welled in her eyes. She blurted out, "You're the one who works and travels like a dog all week; you have a maid, and you told me once that you sometimes still scrub toilets and run the vacuum on the weekends at your house! It's a place to live, not a museum! Sounds like you have a problem too. You should be exhausted just like me. I was just asking for a little empathy, James." I responded, "When I take extra care of my blessings, that is my way of thanking the universe. "The more grateful I am, the more my blessings will be multiplied. By polishing my blessings, above and beyond the work of my housekeeper, I am thanking the universe and demonstrating that I have the capacity for even more blessings. Gratitude is in my heart. Nothing is taken for granted. As a good shepherd of my blessings, the universe is guaranteed to bless me with more."

> The way you are in one area is usually the way you are in all areas. If you've been blocking yourself from receiving money, chances are you've been blocking yourself from receiving anything else that's good in life… The mind has a habit of overgeneralizing and says, "The way it is, is the way it is, everywhere and always."
>
> —T. Harv Ecker

My passionate exchange with Sheryl poignantly reminded me that like the downward spirals of many people, her business's stagnation, along with her plateaued net worth, was attributed to: 1) her bad attitude, 2) her failure to demonstrate the capacity to handle more blessings, and 3) her complete and utter lack of gratitude.

Today, I am proud to report that the tough conversation that Sheryl and I had was a turning point for her. She has grown her company and has acquired another one. The fire is back in her belly, and she is having fun with life. She is not pouting. She is taking care of her blessings. To top it all off, when Sheryl fixed her attitude, she attracted a good man into her life and recently got married. Score!

> A great attitude becomes a great day, which becomes a great month, which becomes a great year, which becomes a great life.
>
> —*Mandy Hale*

As I have discussed all throughout this book, we already know that we must always do the work. As we do the work, we must remember that the universe is *not* finite. There are far more than enough blessings to go around for all of us, with much left over. Remember: the word *blessing* is just another word for responsibility. A key to receiving more is understanding the simple rule that increased blessings are tantamount to increased responsibility. The more things you are blessed with, whether they are material or non-material, the more effort is required for you to care for and nourish those blessings to make them sustainable.

Failure to say *thank you* without cease and to care for what you already have is a guaranteed roadblock to receiving more. The universe is an omnipresent observer of our actions—constantly acknowledging our effort and respecting our internal barometer for capacity. Author and motivator Brendon Burchard reminds us that to receive positive energy, we must give it. He asks, "Are you adding positive energy to your everyday world? How many times did you say thank you this week? Did you make people smile because that was your goal? Did you cheer people on, even those you don't agree with? Did you make others feel appreciated and adored? Did you champion kindness?" Reflect upon his words, and like Sheryl, make some changes in your life, because you can never be too grateful or too positive.

Just as it did for Sheryl, the universe will treat you as you deserve to be treated. Do the work, demonstrate to the universe that you have the capacity to be expanded in all that you do, manifest genuine gratitude, and you will be increased abundantly.

PURPOSEFUL MILLIONAIRE POWER PLAY

1. I want you to get really serious about this next exercise. The point of it is for you to assess whether you are blocking the universe's ability to expand you and bring more blessings into your life. Here we go...

    a. Take a five-minute tour of your home to assess its condition. Be honest with yourself, and rate the condition of your home on a scale of one to five (with five being the highest possible score). For example, if your home is treated like a pigpen or you see dust bunnies the size of live bunny rabbits and piles of dirty clothes scattered across your floors, then give yourself a score of one or two on the cleanliness scale, and so on. You get the point.

        i.   Cleanliness _____

        ii. Orderliness _____

        iii. Scent _____

        iv. Visual Appeal _____

     v. Overall Functionality of Appliances and
        Furniture _____

  b. If you score a three or below in any of the areas
     above, then you may indeed be blocking some of
     the blessings that the universe has intended for
     you. By not caring for your home, which is a per-
     fect reflection of you, or any other things in your
     life with which the universe has already blessed
     you, you are blocking the universe's power to
     bring additional abundance into your life. You
     have demonstrated that you do not care for what
     you have; therefore, you will not receive more. If
     you scored four or above in all of the above cat-
     egories, then you have opened the door to more
     abundance, more responsibility, and more bless-
     ings. You have told the universe, "I am ready, I
     appreciate what you have given me, and I can
     ably care for more!"

2. Repeat out loud five times, "I have everything that
    it takes to be healthy, wealthy, and happy. I am a
    Purposeful Millionaire."

PART III
THE EXECUTION
IDEA + PLAN + *EXECUTION* = SUCCESS

CHAPTER TEN

ACT NOW–THE UNIVERSE IS WAITING ON YOU

I LOVE THE fact that the first three letters of my last name spell the word *Now*: to say my last name is to say my philosophy. Each time I sign a check or ink my name on a contract, I am reminded that life happens in the "now;" I do not dwell on the challenges and failures of the past, but on the power of the present. The *now* is where I always keep my thoughts so that I am fully activated and present in everything that I do in my life. Now is about focus. I say all that because here is what I know for sure: if one fails to live and act in the present, meaning in the *now*, then opportunity for advancement will certainly be lost.

What do you think about when you hear or read the word *now*? Because of its power, *now* can sometimes not be fully appreciated. It is defined as "in the present moment" and is "used especially in conversation to draw attention to a particular statement or point of view." When you act in the *now*, you create motion in your mind, your body, and your spirit. Motion is the potion for emotion, and emotion creates the fire in the belly for action. Once the powerful forces of mind, body, and spirit get moving, they tend to stay in motion. Think about Newton's first law (an object at rest tends to stay at rest, and an object in motion tends to stay in motion). It applies to physics as well as life. People who sit on the sofa eating bonbons and Doritos all day tend to stay stuck on the sofa eating bonbons and Doritos; people who get out into the world and take positive action tend to continue taking positive action.

Be a radical force for change in this world by showing up—by living and acting in the *now*. This means getting out there and executing your plan. Not everyone has the strength or courage to do this, but you can. The universe is waiting on you to show up so that it can reward you. In this chapter, I am going to share with you some specific examples about how living in the *now*, or in other words, executing and not looking back, has worked for me.

Rule #26: You must live and act in the now so that when opportunity presents itself, you can seize it.

On countless occasions in my business affairs and personal life, had I not acted quickly when provided with an opportunity, the chance to increase myself would have been passed on to someone else. I know that when opportunity falls into my lap, I must act upon it quickly, or that opportunity could become someone else's blessing.

You may remember the African proverb that I mentioned earlier: "When you say a prayer, move your feet." Don't just sit there and ask or beg the universe for something. Do something about it right now. By stalling with analysis paralysis, opportunity fades and luck dissipates. Acting upon opportunity requires courage. It requires having faith in yourself. If you, like many, do not find the courage to act, you will be SOL. Your life will be the same. The bus of abundance will drive right past you.

In any given moment of decision, the best thing you can do is the right thing, the next best thing is the wrong thing, and the worst thing you can do is nothing.

—*Theodore Roosevelt*

It takes bravery to act when the opportunity is ripe; however, I believe that if you risk nothing, you gain nothing. By acting upon opportunity, you set the universe in motion to become activated, moving energy everywhere to ensure that the proper forces are in place for success. Folks have looked at me thinking how lucky I am. They are right. I am darn *lucky*. I created my luck. I took the doggone risks. The risks included putting myself through college, a year of medical school, and three years of law school with part-time work and student loans; skirting the edges of bankruptcy during the Great Recession; starting an enterprise with virtually no capital for seed money; using the roof over my head as a line of credit for my business's growth; and never shrinking from my identity as a great businessman, who just happens to be a happily married gay man of color, in every boardroom or corporation that I have ever walked into. I could go on and on, but what I know is that all these risks took some serious courage.

Over time, I would grow the great muscle of courage and develop a higher tolerance for risk and reward and grace under pressure that would lead to positive action after positive action. What I know is that by acting in the now, the universe rewarded me for loving myself and for wanting more for myself; and that the universe will multiply those rewards for me again and again so long as I live true to my habits and value system. I got exactly what I asked for, and much of that achievement is due to thanking my Creator without cease, while being exquisitely authentic about how He made me.

> Be yourself; everyone else is already taken.
>
> —*Oscar Wilde*

Had I wasted time doubting myself or wondering what other people thought of me or living someone else's dream for me, I would never have gotten as far. If I could give my younger self one piece of advice, it would be this: ***Don't Compete. Be Unique.*** Being inauthentic is an absolute waste of energy. Focusing on haters or their discouragement will never get them to like you. Don't squander any energy on them. They do not live in the now like you. They live in the past, with minds stuck in the sands of self-created limitations and envy of why they are not succeeding as well as you. Remember to stay focused on yourself, be yourself, wish haters well, and don't get distracted. Just as I learned to do, you can take the high road too.

> If I didn't define myself for myself, I would be crunched into other people's fantasies for me and eaten alive.
>
> –*Audre Lorde*

Sometimes acting upon opportunity will not turn into blessings. Don't be scared of that—that's life. But acting upon opportunity *will* motivate you to get your hind parts off of the sofa. It will get you moving and prepared to be present so that opportunity can meet you where you are.

Rule #27: Acting upon opportunity
does not always end favorably. But
when you fall, fall forward.

Also, sometimes acting upon opportunity will bring you bad luck—that's also life, and it's kind of crappy. However, more often than not, action will lead to more doors of opportunity opening for you, eventually escalating your life to the next level and beyond. Just keep bouncing back, and keep on moving forward. Each time you have a setback, work on getting your mind in such a good place that each time you fall in life you fall forward, just like in yoga practice, and get back up even more quickly the next time. It's easy to say that, but it is hard to do. I am rooting for you!

Imagine a brilliant entrepreneur who aspires to own his own business yet lacks the courage and confidence to leave the comforts of his home to pursue clients—and thus, opportunity. Perhaps he thinks that he is not articulate, smart, likeable, funny, handsome, charming, or personable enough to mingle with successful folks at a fancy cocktail party. Maybe he thinks he is too brown, too poor and white, too black, too gay, too unworldly, too inarticulate, too unrefined, too country, too unsophisticated. You get the point. He believes that he is not worthy of being in the room. All of those limiting factors were created in his mind to trap him in a cage of mediocrity, self-bondage, and self-doubt.

One day that man—or a man like him—receives an invitation from a co-worker to attend a seminar and decides to show up. He walks into the room and, though nervous wreck at first, connects with a couple of other people who are equally as nervous and full of self-doubt. He cracks a few dry jokes, and before he knows it, he has made several new friends—one of whom will make a critical introduction to another businessman in the room who will eventually become his business partner.

Five years later, the two partners have built a respected multimillion-dollar enterprise. Just imagine if that man full of self-doubt had stayed at home. *Imagine if he had not acted in the now.* He took the risk of showing up and received the benefit. That man, an introvert at heart, is a dear friend of mine and has just completed the Series B round of funding for his company for eleven million dollars.

> Be willing to be uncomfortable. Be comfortable being uncomfortable. It may be tough, but it's a small price to pay for living a dream.
>
> —Peter McWilliams

When I launched Excel Global Partners years ago, I had not one consulting client and no dollars coming in the door. Zero. Zip. Nada. As I discussed earlier, the exciting launch of my firm was a precursor to a market crash, the housing crisis, and the Great Recession, the worst the U.S. economy had performed since the Great Depression. Times were scary. During this time, I asked myself, "Why in the world did I leave my comfortable salary? What was I smoking?" The truth was that no one, other than a few insiders on Wall Street (well, maybe quite a few insiders on Wall

Street) saw the economic crash coming. But not I, and certainly not my friends.

Needless to say, with my savings quickly diminishing, I was scared out of my mind, but I knew that all I needed was a little opportunity to keep the lights on. Naïveté aside, I had to pull myself together, not worry about the past, and focus on acting NOW. I am sure glad I did.

> No matter how much you revisit the past there is nothing new to see.
>
> —*Robert Tew*

During the challenging time of launching my firm, for several weeks straight, I called the number of every business that I could find listed in the business journals of Dallas, Houston, and Austin. I had the good sense to know that when some businesses struggle during a down economy, others thrive.

Rule #28: Allow your setbacks to open
the biggest doors for your future.

I wanted to find that golden egg—I just knew it was out there. During my calls, many people hung up on me. Others expressed frustration at my soliciting. A few of them preached at me: "Who do you think would buy your consulting services during this crappy economy. We are barely keeping the lights on!" In spite of these rejections, I did not give up. I kept dialing. I faced losing everything I had worked for, and especially my pride if I did not find a client ASAP. I needed an opportunity now!

Late one Tuesday evening, well after business hours, a little voice in my head told me to make one more phone call. I did. Because it was after hours, the receptionist at the business I called had forwarded the switchboard to the C-suite. Lucky me. BINGO! BINGO! BINGO! This was my big break. A man with a gruff voice answered the call. "Yeah?" No hello, just "yeah?"

My heart almost jumped out of my chest. My palms were sweating so much that I almost dropped the phone. I stammered, "S-s-sir, th-this is James Nowlin, CEO of Excel Global Partners, a corporate consulting firm that helps companies like yours improve financial and operational performance." He interrupted and puffed, "Yeah, and what do you need from me? Do you know how late it is?" I pulled myself together to say something that I hope was intelligible, and the conversation continued. I thought I was talking to a royal turnip and was ready to hang up. Fortunately, my momma had raised me always to take the high road. "Kill them with kindness," she would say. Following her advice, I politely asked him to talk to me in detail about his business and some of the challenges that it might be facing. He opened up and explained. I listened. Eureka! I had gotten the man with the gruff voice to have a conversation with me.

Little did I know at the time, my company was exactly what this CEO was looking for. A highly accomplished man leading a family enterprise with revenues greater than $250 million, he saw something in little unseasoned me and told me to meet him at his office the next day. The following day, I put on my best suit and tie, collected my nerves, dried off my sweaty palms, and we met: I, a man in my twenties, and he, a man in his sixties, with different interests, life experiences, and backgrounds. We could not have been more different. But we instantly formed a connection over the goals of his business. I had unearthed common ground. I had found a client. Hallelujah!

Three months later after completing a number of long-range strategic planning initiatives for this new client, I received a check in the mail for $44,375 with a handwritten note saying "Well done!" This money not only saved my pride and my personal life but also would become the seed funds for building a much larger company.

Rule #29: Execution is nearly everything. Take the first step in spite of fear, and the universe will give you the courage that you need to continue each step of your journey.

This feat had whet my appetite for more. I was humbled and beyond grateful. If not for my making that one phone call and acting in the now, the trajectory of my business and my life could have been much different. Because I acted, in spite of fear, the universe had taken care of me. I would now not be afraid to pick up the phone and articulate the value proposition of Excel Global Partners. I was ready to dial for more dollars! I went beyond my discomfort, fears, and self-judgment. I was ready for more.

Life begins at the edge of your comfort zone.

—*Neale Donald Walsh*

Execution is what separates the big dogs from those who stay at home, or better yet, from those who never leave the front porch. The lesson of which I have been reminded time and again from experience is that acting now, even when it feels uncomfortable or unnatural, sets the universe in motion for further motion. This law of inertia and of life creates a force field of opportunity. Confidence, and also luck, build on that journey up the stairwell, but neither one would come if not for your taking the first step.

Dr. King talked about this kind of courage when he said, "Take the first step in faith. You don't have to see the whole staircase; just take the first step." For me, his words give me the encouragement I need to stop doubting myself and to get out there and execute in the now. What I have learned is that though the first step is the most daunting, each step along the way gets easier. That's the beauty of courage. We just have to take the first step for the universe to begin responding.

With sweaty palms and all, I had found my start. I had taken my first step. I had learned the lesson that a life of great opportunity happens only in the *now*. Fully present and actualized, with great respect for the extraordinary power of execution, in spite of all fears, I would cherish this mantra of *now*. I know that it will surely lead me to greater success for the rest of my life. I am ready.

PURPOSEFUL MILLIONAIRE POWER PLAY

1. Dreams will never come true if they are not acted upon. Procrastination is the killer of all dreams. Write down your number one goal and list the reasons why you have procrastinated executing that goal. Can you see that none of these excuses is valid? Can you see that the only thing that has been holding

you back has been yourself? How does this make you feel? Repeat out loud five times, "I have everything that it takes to be healthy, wealthy, and happy. I am a Purposeful Millionaire."

2. The author and motivator Tim Ferriss asks his readers, "What would you do to accomplish your ten-year plan in six months if you had a gun to your head?" This question reminds us of the power of now and how procrastination and slow movement can decelerate our lives. Take a moment to reflect upon your goals and answer these questions. Are you moving too slowly; do you doubt yourself; is that doubt slowing down your execution; what could you do to accelerate your plan?

3. Repeat out loud five times, "I have everything that it takes to be healthy, wealthy, and happy. I am a Purposeful Millionaire."

CHAPTER ELEVEN

LIFE CAN BE UNFAIR– MAKE IT FAIR FOR YOU

MY DREAMS HAD to get bigger than my excuses for me to achieve any success in life. You know enough about me now that you are aware that things have not been perfect and that people have not always been perfectly fair to me, but what guided me through it all was my positive mindset and relentless work ethic. That being said, the game of life is indeed unfair, and many people have had great cause to affirm it as such.

The game of life probably seemed unfair to Abraham Lincoln who had little formal education; lost his mother, sister, and two of his sons all at a young age; suffered a nervous breakdown at twenty-seven; was defeated for Congress at thirty-four; and defeated for Senate at forty-six and forty-nine; Stephen Hawking who was paralyzed by Lou Gehrig's disease and cannot speak; Oprah Winfrey who gave birth at age fourteen and lost her child; Colonel Sanders who failed 1009 times before selling his recipe for KFC; Albert Einstein who did not speak until he was four years old; J. K. Rowling who once lived on welfare; Bill Gates whose first business failed; Jay-Z who was rejected by countless record labels before launching his career; Charlize Theron who as a child witnessed her mother shoot her alcoholic father in self-defense; Mellody Hobson who overcame being a woman of color in an industry dominated by men; Richard Branson who has dyslexia; Franklin D. Roosevelt who was paralyzed from the waist down on account of polio; Justice Sonia Sotomayor who grew up in a working-class family in the Bronx and whose intellect and work ethic paved the way for her as the first Latina on the U.S. Supreme Court; or Thomas Edison who failed more than a thousand times before inventing the light bulb. These great individuals illustrate the boundless power of the mind and the fact that the game is not rigged. Opportunity and success are available for anyone despite any obstacle.

I have not failed. I've just found ten thousand ways that won't work.

—*Thomas Edison*

Like the high-achievers and legends mentioned above, you will not be completely free until you are master of your mind, which leads to mastery of your universe. Until then, you will be an indentured servant to self-minimizing thoughts and doubts, which will lead to a life of ho-hum mediocrity. Of course, you do not want that for yourself because you are reading this book. To overcome a life of mediocrity, you must understand that mastery of your universe requires acceptance of the very laws that are perfectly styled by history and accepted by those who have achieved at extraordinary levels. This chapter is about accepting some essential realities about life and mastering the rules of success that have been laid out in this book, or what we call "the game."

The game is not rigged. It is tested by time and always expanding. The game does, however, become increasingly complicated the higher one gets on the stairwell. The game is not always fair and certainly not always easy. If the game were easy, then everyone would be a success story. And, quite frankly, people who are not willing to master the game and do the work do not deserve to be success stories. If the contrary were the case, then great opportunity would fall into the laps of those who did not deserve it. That alone is an injustice in and of itself.

The game is complex and full of trip wires and stumbling blocks that require resilience, an open mind, humility, perseverance, and strength. Being at the top is complicated, much more complicated than most dreamers would ever imagine. But being at the top, with all its challenges, can be fun and incredibly rewarding. The top requires inexhaustible amounts of energy, strategy, endurance, street and business smarts, and wit. The top darn sure requires that each person pay his or her dues to be there; otherwise, without fail, the universe may abruptly correct the order in due time.

> Man became free when he recognized that he was subject to law.
>
> —*Will Durant*

Nobody ever promised anyone that the game would be easy or fun. The game of success requires a mastery of the rules—and not all the rules are fair. Some people seem to think that there is a shortcut or a way to get around the basic tenets of life and success, but there are no shortcuts. Those folks who attempt to outthink the rules of the game often end up at the bottom. The universe rewards strategy, authenticity, and hard work. Unsuccessful people avoid the very tools that the universe has been using to try to change them. They believe that there is an elevator that will float them all the way to the top. In fact, they may spend years, even decades, working on their plan to actually find the elevator. This is a waste of time. Successful people take the stairs.

Rule #30: Life is not always fair. Make it fair for you by accepting the rules of the game and acting upon them.

The first step to mastering the rules is to accept the fact that not all the rules are fair. I often tell people, "I didn't invent the game of creating success or its rules. I have just learned how to play!" This initial acceptance of the game is the biggest hurdle to overcome. By accepting the rules, you are not reinventing the wheel; you are embracing the laws of the universe, freeing your energy to focus on what matters most: your future. Fairness of the game is in the eye of the beholder. But the universe will reward you if you accept the rules of its game. Those who only dream or fail and refuse to get back up will always see the game as rigged. There have been many ignorant people who spend their energy on questioning the degree to which the system is rigged. Just ignore them. They will never master the game.

Unlike the successful men and women mentioned in this chapter, many people spend more time trying to reinvent or reconfigure the laws of the world than they do trying to overcome their very own inertia. Sometimes these people spend their entire lives stuck playing their own personal game, but not the universe's game. This results in a life of little achievement and minimal self-mastery. There have been very few cases in history in which anyone was able to successfully recreate the game. In addition to not fully accepting the laws of the universe, when one is miseducated about relationships, power, access to power, money, opportunity, and privilege, one may never escape his or her current situation.

> The universe will bless you and keep you out of trouble if you honor it.
>
> *—Unknown*

The most successful people glide through the bumps and hiccups of life with grace and style, rarely allowing others to see them sweat. That is because they have accepted the rules of the universe and understand how the game is played. In spite of their stress levels, they are more focused on properly handling their affairs and mastering their ideas, rather than on trying to reinvent the rules that they have learned throughout their lives.

Take Warren Buffett, Bill Gates, and Robert Smith (a neighbor of mine and a multi-billionaire who happens to be black) for example. I can assure you that all of them are constantly reading, researching, and brainstorming new ideas and opportunities; however, you won't find them spinning their wheels attempting to recreate the many rules of the universe. When it comes to dealing with the universe, they play the cards that they have been dealt, not dwelling on the past but embracing the rules and spending their energy on expansion, not on alteration of the simple rules of the game. To top it all off, this approach to life keeps people like Buffett, Gates, and Smith out of the weeds, and it certainly keeps them out of trouble.

Other people who get to the top by trying to bend the rules often eventually end up on the cover of newspapers—usually in a notorious kind of way. Once ill fame is achieved, all the goodwill that one has created in the universe dissipates. Buffett, Gates, and Smith know that not all press is good press. So a lesson learned from them: respect the rules of the game, and guard your reputation like a fortress. Protect it at all costs.

> This is not a haphazard universe in which you live. It is a very well-defined, perfectly organized universe. Your only work is to get in alignment with the perfection of it, which means that you must believe that all is well, and in the moment that you believe all is well—everything that touches you is well.
>
> —*Abraham Hicks*

We all should commit time to learning more about how masters of the game like Buffett, Gates, and Smith approach business and life. In addition to reading this book, you should be spending time reading about the success stories of other people and the philosophies that they hold dearly. We could learn a lot from them, especially if we are interested in listening and learning, instead of figuring out how to take the elevator to the top, which some people seem determined to do.

One day I was speaking with a young entrepreneur regarding his approach to launching his business. He spent more time trying to convince me, a seasoned businessman, about some shortcuts that he was attempting and why the business was destined to be an instant success than on talking about the actual concept and strategy of his business. I hear these kinds of conversations all the time from people who are new to business and who underestimate the extraordinary complexity of the game. In so many words, I kindly urged him to slow down and to do things right, step by step, and to seek the proper resources for building the foundation of his business.

Though he may have taken my advice as being overly critical, it was my duty to share with him that there are no shortcuts and that, first, a certain game must be mastered. To this day, I periodically check his profile to see how his online business is doing. The name of the URL that he gave me remains unregistered. He did not wish to listen, to learn, or to play by the rules of the game. He probably had to learn the hard way that shortcuts do not work.

From inception all the way through the long journey of success, there are few shortcuts. Relationships cannot be forced; businesses cannot avoid proper marketing; taxes and accounting cannot be ignored; legal and organizational documents and processes cannot be skirted around; leaders cannot dwell in the past; nothing can succeed without a plan or the right internal infrastructure and controls. All these things are true.

The world is an extremely complex place. Business, personal performance, and success are equally complex. They require work—lots of it. This stuff ain't easy at all, y'all. Just cling to these facts about the rules and don't run from them or try to recreate them. Embrace the universe, and watch the universe work for you!

PURPOSEFUL MILLIONAIRE POWER PLAY

1. Write down all of the thoughts and sayings that you have heard throughout your life about money, why the game is rigged, and perhaps why rich people take advantage of others to be rich. Reflect upon whether these thoughts are serving you. Reflect upon whether you accept the rules of the game or whether you have been wasting your energy working against the rules of the game. Say out loud five times, "To be a healthy, wealthy, and happy Purposeful Millionaire, I must first accept the rules of the game. Once I accept the rules and begin to do the work, the universe will become unequivocally rigged in my favor."

2. Repeat out loud five times, "I have everything that it takes to be healthy, wealthy, and happy. I am a Purposeful Millionaire."

CHAPTER TWELVE

GREAT SACRIFICES TODAY, GREAT REWARDS TOMORROW

Never give up on a dream just because of the time it will take to accomplish it. The time will pass anyway.

—*Earl Nightingale*

AS AN AMERICAN, I have a duty to share what I have learned and to open up certain conversations about success—to throw them into the air and pray that the wind catches them and that at least five, fifty, or perhaps a million people can effect change because of these lessons learned and how candidly I speak about them. I do not ignore the fact that when society tells people to pick themselves up by their bootstraps, some have no boots at all. They don't even have flip-flops. Their path toward achievement is nearly impossible. They are barefooted and must rely on their fellow comrade to lift them up. I write, speak, and mentor so that the secrets of success will not be hoarded or hidden from them or anyone, for that matter. That is my calling.

The secrets must be open to all—from the disenfranchised Republican of coal country, Appalachia; to the Hispanic immigrant of Texas; to the destitute Native American in the hills of Oklahoma; to the black youth of Gary, Indiana. My belief is that intrinsically very few of these people want a handout. They simply want a hand to help them up.

While at a summer program during my first or second year in college, I had the good fortune to hear some powerful words from a surgeon at a top Chicago hospital that would stick with me for the rest of my life. Little did I know at the time, the words would be the foundation upon which I would ground my thoughts for the remainder of my years in college and graduate school. By hearing, reflecting upon, writing down, and cherishing the mantra that he shared with us about how he overcame challenging circumstance, "Live like no one else will for a few years so that you can live like no one else can for the rest of your life," I had been taught more in one sentence than I would learn in some of my classes.

Once I had heard that advice, I quickly returned to my dorm room to type the words out on my computer so that I could print them out. I then taped them to my monitor, where they would stay until graduation.

Each day as I studied and wrote at my computer, a simple glance at those words would program my subconscious for success. My subconscious would think in terms of making the right decisions, synthesizing my ideas and plans about my future positively and systematically, and grounding myself in the determination of a college student who would be the first member of his family to one day achieve at the highest levels. While other students were partying and exploring their youth, unmentionable indiscretions included (though I too did some immature acts as a youth), true to the words taped to my computer screen, I was burning the midnight oil by burying myself in my coursework. This focus created a less-than-exciting university experience but a sparkling transcript that would later open doors for me. I knew that to earn more, I had to learn more.

At college, I could easily see that some of my classmates had a head start on me. Others had more challenges than I had and came from circumstances much worse than mine. I did not waste my time comparing myself to anyone, but I became stubbornly-bent on surpassing them all and especially determined to achieve the personal roadmap that I had created for my future career, wealth, family, and happiness.

Folks might have found me competitive, including some professors who I am sure tired of my asking questions and overstaying my welcome during office hours. But I was on a critical mission. The mission was to lay a new foundation above the limitations that I had learned growing up in Lynchburg, so that I could be the first in my family to live like no one else would for a few years so that I could live like no one else could for the rest of my life. I knew, however, that this change in values and lifestyle would take a lot more than working hard in the classroom. An essential extracurricular reprogramming of the mind would be required.

Rule #31: Prepare yourself for change as you climb the stairwell of social class. The differences between one social class and another and each one's rules of the game, subtle as they may seem, are tremendous.

I aspired not only to depart from my working-class existence but also to achieve eventual membership into the highest class.

When moving from one class to another, one must change many aspects of oneself, including posture, language, hobbies, personal networks, travel decisions, and life interests.

The differences between one social class and another, subtle as they may seem, are tremendous. I would never forget where I came from, but I always knew exactly where I was going. I studied the lessons and value systems learned at each level. And through practice and some social hiccups along the way, I learned the great power of being able to traverse various hierarchies of class structure, race, and social mores on a whim. This is not inauthentic. This is called street skills and the power of being incredibly versatile, the power of being true to myself from the backwoods to Beverly Hills—or as some would say, from the outhouse to the White House. Each experience I have in life I take with me, and each experience is part of who I am.

This great versatility and these stylistic changes did not happen overnight. Along the way, I would be reminded of what I already knew: money will not buy class. It usually never does. Money can advance one only so far in the hierarchy of class; attitude and mindset are what ultimately determine how far one can go. One does not have to look very far to see this rule in effect.

I would also be brutally reminded that in the eyes of some ignorant people, but many fewer than I once imagined as a young man, race would be the permanent, immobile determiner of my designation of class, not achievement or character. In spite of those fools, countless people of many backgrounds have liked me and loved me. I am grateful for that. I earned their trust, and they opened doors for me. In the America that I created for myself, people whose trust, respect, and love I earned were black, white, and every shade in between. In my America, and in my cautiously trained and fiercely optimistic mind, there is no glass ceiling. I refuse to believe otherwise.

People get stuck in their places in the social order. We are all born into a class, and when people work hard to achieve a change in social class, that is no small feat. Their accomplishments and social elevation required vision, adjustments, and persistence. This change for them also required mastery of self as well as of people. Others' perceptions, social cues, slights, and prejudices all had to be properly acknowledged and duly noted.

Some Americans simply cannot break through to effect change in themselves, and others all too readily accept their place. Class, social order, wealth, language, dress, and the subtleties of social cues are simply not talked about. They are pariahs. We do not discuss things like that because we are all "equal," right? Nothing could be farther from the truth, and that is the exact pain that people take with them to the voting box. The false acceptance of this dreamed-up reality of equality is very unsettling. This lack of awareness is particularly problematic as we try to excavate the roots of injustice for women, people of color, poor whites, gay folks, people of certain religions, and other minorities. It is troubling that people believe we are all equal by birth. Do not believe the hype. But we are all American and have license to stand up and create our equality.

Though I had no idea where certain decisions would take me, after grinding it out for nearly a decade as an adult on my own in college and graduate studies, I began to achieve a life beyond anything that the hills of Virginia, in what was almost Appalachia, could offer—a life that was more than a new shiny pickup truck and fledgling mediocrity at best.

Rule #32: Realize the extent to which your
environment matters. You must realize that
before you can accurately assess your own
situation. Get the hell out if necessary.

During my teenaged years, I held a number of odd jobs. I worked as the weekend janitor at my parents' jukejoint-rumpshaking-fistfighting-malt-liquor-serving-nightclub called OJ's in a crime-ridden part of town called White Rock (near the Greenfield housing projects) that we did not live in, but I knew well. I had gone to elementary school and rode the bus with the kids who lived there, so that part of town was the basis of my most formative years. It was not the janitor job at the juke joint in White Rock, but another job that I held in the area that I reflect the most fondly upon—it was caring for the yard of a wise senior citizen, Mrs. Mineola Trudy Chase, not too far away in a relatively more prosperous neighboring area. Conversations with her would plant a seed in my mind that I could be and do more than my small hometown would ever permit.

Mrs. Chase's husband had recently died, and she considered herself a learned, refined individual—which she was. She always dreamed of more than what the hills of Virginia could offer. In fact, she was one of the few black women of her generation in our town to earn a college education; she was a highly respected chemistry teacher, vocal church parishioner, and community volunteer. She and I developed a special relationship, and she always encouraged me to do my absolute best and to be more than what Lynchburg could ever offer me. I liked her and she liked me. She saw something in me that she had once seen in herself—the sparkle in my eyes about wanting the absolute most that life could offer.

One day, after I had finished cutting Mrs. Chase's grass and trimming the hedges, she sat me down on the front stoop of her house and told me that she needed to talk to me. Since she was known for her forwardness, once again, I was wondering what kind of blunt advice she would be offering me that day. Geez, what had I gotten myself into? This old woman, I thought, was going to be preaching to me for hours. Let me go grab my water thermos and make myself comfortable on her stoop.

Mrs. Chase said, "JR (my childhood nickname), you are different and you are special." Boy was she right about that! To my surprise, she asserted, "Just make one promise to me. Put on a condom, and never get one of these hoochie girls around here knocked up! They will even take a pin and prick a hole in a condom so that they can have a baby by a young man like you. You know you're handsome and highly intelligent, right? A lot of folks are looking at you, including those hoochies. And a lot of folks will try to hurt you. Watch yourself, baby."

Feeling a little insulted—I was not sexually active and was way too focused on my books at the time (and little did Mrs. Chase or I know back then, I don't roll that way anyway!)—I thought, okay, is that all this woman has to tell me? Why did she sit me down for a talk about the birds and the bees? I had already learned about how body parts work and what condoms do in middle school in Sex Ed or "Family Life" as they called it back then. As a teenager, I was not planning on "knocking up" anything other than the highest scores I could possibly achieve on the SAT as well as some A's on my report card.

After what seemed like an endless rant, she sipped her lemonade and continued, dropping more *knowledge bombs* on me, "Once you leave here, you must never come back! Get the hell out and stay out. There is more opportunity in the world than you can imagine if you would just leave and stay gone. Let your roots grow elsewhere." I thought this woman had lost her mind. What in the world was going on? This was Mrs. Mineola Trudy Chase—talking to me about sex and some random hoochie girls putting pinholes in my condoms. Now she was telling me to run away from home. Say what? Had she bumped her ever-loving head?

Mrs. Chase's advice was scary, but it was sound. My hometown was really all that I knew, and as a teenager, I did not understand what she was talking about. At the time, I had dreamed about living a bigger life somewhere else. Still, in Lynchburg, I thought we had everything that I would ever need. But I would learn later in life that my environment was ill-equipped to give me what I was looking for and further ill equipped to allow me to fulfill my potential.

Mrs. Chase shared with me many of the dreams she had had in her younger life. She had accomplished a great deal in life for a woman of her generation, but she was still hungry for more, even if that would be achieved simply by witnessing me on the path of increase. She grew up during a period in which there had been an urgent need for achievement planted in the minds of black people as the doors of opportunity opened after Jim Crow slowly fell. She would share with me some of her regrets and some of the challenges that she had overcome. Most of all, she would share with me her wisdom that our lives are much shorter than we think.

In her late sixties at the time, she knew that she had already lived most of the years of her life and that, as a retired woman, a new career was not exactly on the table. Mrs. Chase's words stick with me to this day; they planted the seed in my mind that I could be and do more and that the environment in which I lived could certainly play a role in the limitation or the expansion of my dreams. I thank her for that. Last I heard, Mrs. Chase, in her eighties today, has relocated to North Carolina and is just as preachy and vibrant as ever. My hope is that she is continuing to drop knowledge bombs on other youth like she did on me.

∽

Many people go through their lives with their fingers crossed, hoping that each haphazard day something better will happen to them. By crossing their fingers each day for good luck or opportunity, they fail to put any plan in place to increase themselves or their chances for a journey to any semblance of prosperity. They are satisfied—or at least satisfied enough to be willing to do only the work of committing to buying lottery tickets at the neighborhood gas station. Lacking the critical combination of courage and willpower to change our circumstances can ruin us. By staying in our comfort zone, such as in the familiarity of where we grew up in our little hometown, we can cut off our dreams before they ever get started.

Rule #33: Familiarity and comfort are overrated. Do not get trapped in a comfortable existence because nothing great is ever achieved in comfort.

If necessary, you must accept the limitations of your environment and find a different place to spread your wings. Reinventing or pushing the boundaries or capabilities of your environment is essentially impossible. There are thousands of places in the world that are a fit for you and your dreams. The world is enormous, and there is a special place for you and your dreams somewhere. As you evaluate your environment and the situation in which you find yourself, are there examples of abundance in your immediate community for people who dream as big as you? Do your surroundings encourage you or discourage you? Do you feel trapped by the small-mindedness of the people where you live? Are you a diamond trapped inside a lump of coal? If any of these things are true, force change to happen in your life, knowing that change will be hard and complicated, but that through purposeful change, you can direct yourself, heal yourself, and create a much richer, fuller, and happier life.

Someone once said that middle-class people think that being comfortable is the ultimate goal and that comfort means being happy. Self-made rich people, on the other hand, know that taking risks and being uncomfortable mean that extraordinary results may ensue from that discomfort. Getting the hell out of my hometown by heeding the sage advice of an elder took a giant leap of faith. When I was seventeen, leaving home to go to college, a mere hour and fifteen minutes' drive north through the hills of Virginia, was one of the most courageous things that I had done. It was worth it.

When I told people that I was going to be attending the University of Virginia, some nonchalantly said, "Oh, okay. Cool." Others said, "Wow! I am so proud of you. I know you will do well." Others asked why was I so gung ho on leaving home. By having the courage to leave, I would find that my world would expand to include travel to nearly all fifty states and more than thirty countries around the world, and the number is growing. My eventual rise would also include the addition of many zeros to my financial account balances. And my world expands each year–I like that–this stuff is some serious fun. As my world expanded, reflecting upon Mrs. Chase's words gave me strength. She knew what she was talking about.

✌

Going back to day one of arriving at college, within forty-eight hours of being dropped off by my family, I could only think: "What the ham sandwich have I gotten myself into? I do not belong here!" From a town sixty-something miles southwest of UVA, my hick self was culture shocked. At one of the nation's top universities, surrounded by world-class professors and students in the halls of elite academia, I was completely out of my element. Lucky for me, I had chosen an institution that was stellar, though before my arrival, I barely knew the difference between UVA and Podunk State. I just knew that people whom I considered smart always talked about UVA a lot and that I thought Monticello (Thomas Jefferson's homestead near UVA) was pretty cool—I had visited it while in high school. I consider landing at UVA a stroke of good luck. The universe was looking out for me.

Though I had not been fully prepared for my arrival at the university, my high school and amazing teachers had given me a solid start, the educational foundation that I needed to succeed academically. More important, my view of life opened to a greater world at UVA. It was as if someone had turned on the lights. Given what UVA was and what it had to offer, including student organizations, internship opportunities, a world-class peer advisory program led by legendary Associate Dean Sylvia Terry, and mentorship by professors and deans who had traveled and studied around the world, my eyes had been opened, and I knew that my education would set me free. After graduating from UVA, my short stint at Howard Med and my three years at Duke Law to earn my juris doctorate would take that eye-opening to a whole 'nother level.

<hr>

Rule #34: Talent without application
is a waste. Use your talent wisely.

<hr>

As a student, I knew that mathematics was not my natural forte. However, I forced myself to take advanced placement math classes all the way up to Calculus II. I busted my chops in those classes and made some A's and mostly B's, but I knew that the rigor of advanced mathematics would sharpen my mind to think beyond its natural gifts. I did not what was comfortable and certainly not what was easy.

As I worked through math coursework, I would sometimes think about a high school friend of mine. We will call him Teddy. He was naturally gifted at math. He could show up for any test without studying and ace it. Laughably, I was the opposite of Teddy when it came to math. To watch him effortlessly fly through algebra, geometry, trigonometry, physics, and calculus was like watching a force of nature.

Teddy loved math, and everyone around him could see a future great professor, mathematician, theorist, engineer, or architect in the making. One day during lunch in high school, I sat down with Teddy and asked, "So Teddy, what do you want to be when you grow up?" He responded, "I'm going to be an inventor." He ticked off a number of things that he had invented and spoke extensively about the prototypes he had created in his garage. As Teddy spoke in detail about the inventions, I just knew that I would be friends with someone famous who would change the world at some point in the foreseeable future. I would have been willing to bet my lunch money to invest in the amazing ideas that he had shared with me.

Nearly twenty years later, Teddy has not accomplished much of anything beyond what he did in high school. His ideas and excited talk have led to not one solitary implementation of an idea or patent for his inventions, and his day job, or rather, his career, has provided nothing more than a basic but relatively comfortable lifestyle for him and his family. Today, Teddy is resigned to "working for the man" at a factory near where he and I grew up. There is absolutely nothing wrong with the life that Teddy lives and has created for himself. He is a decent, tax-paying citizen and a good family man. However, in my opinion, he absolutely did not live up to the plans he bragged about in high school or a fraction of his potential. His big brain gave him a significant head start in this world, and he did not apply it. Call me judgmental, but I have talked with Teddy, and he flat-out realizes that he fell short in the confidence and execution department. I just knew that Teddy would one day be famous, had he taken the first step and just applied himself.

Instead of toughing it out and leaving Lynchburg to work his butt off in college, Teddy took few risks, made few sacrifices, and took a good job with benefits at a local factory, got married and soon thereafter had children. Nothing is entirely wrong with that path, but it has made him live with significant regrets. Thinking that he was doing the right thing at the time, Teddy's father had gotten him on at the factory where he worked for more than twenty years, and Teddy followed in his footsteps. With a job straight out of high school, Teddy was able to start making a full wage as an eighteen-year-old working for the man. While he took the fast route and was making solid middle-class wages (which is honorable in its own right), I would stay focused on coursework, eating ramen noodles, and driving a jalopy, compared to his new, shiny black Nissan, which I secretly coveted at the time.

Teddy's situation is not even a case of a dream's being deferred. It is a failure to apply gifts, a failure to expand upon God-given talents to make the world a better place. I get sad just thinking about how he did not execute his plan and how his big brain is underused. The worst part is that he is still a young man, yet unwilling to apply all of his talents, return to school, or to start some kind of business that could spread his talent with the world. He is comfortable, or so he thinks. As for me, I will squeeze every drop of juice possible out of the talents that the universe has given me. I know that you will do that too.

Rule #35: Recognize your gifts,
and make the sacrifices required to
nurture and develop them fully.

Teddy failed to recognize his gifts, and he certainly failed to make the sacrifices necessary to share those gifts with the world. Teddy had the brain of brains. He most certainly had the ideas. But he lacked the vision (the idea and the plan) and the willpower (steadfast commitment to execution) to succeed.

Long story short, Teddy is like most people insofar as he has not lived up to his potential. Also, like many people, he is jaded by what life and the realities of adulthood have thrown at him, including lots of bills. Adulthood is not child's play. It has its own set of challenges and can throw a person a lot of curveballs. But with a brain like his, Teddy could have been anything he wanted to be. From talking with him, I am not certain that he was willing to make the sacrifices that come with living like no one else will so that he could live like no one else could for the rest of his life. Today, though he and I stay in touch via social media, we have very little in common. There is very little to talk about.

Unlike Teddy's, my first full-time job would come later in life, at the age of twenty-five. My first full-time gig got me on my feet in a way that would alter my life's course beyond what I could ever imagine. My experience, skillset, and compensation would go only higher each subsequent year of my life, and the foundation had been laid for greater opportunity. Teddy, on the other hand, would not arrive. Mediocrity and little risk-taking would pave a mediocre, bill- and debt-laden road for him. I knew that if I risked nothing, I would gain nothing. Taking the risk was hard, but I decided to do it anyway, understanding that delayed gratification is the sweetest of rewards.

Rule #36: Privilege and opportunity are underrated. Opportunity may bring comfort, but comfort will not bring opportunity.

Reflecting on the trajectory of my life in contrast to that of a high school whiz kid reminds me of a few things. First, comfort is overrated, and privilege and opportunity are underrated. Second, mediocrity for me is incredibly boring. Third, ideas are nice to have, and having a plan is even better; but if you fail to execute, the dream will never be achieved. Remember that all three components of the formula must be applied for success or elevation to be achieved:

Idea + Plan + Execution = Success

Or

Motivation + Preparation + Perspiration = Elevation

Execution is where the hard work is done. Lots of people have ideas, some have plans, but few can execute to turn the ideas and plans into success. The rearrangement that takes place in the universe is unfathomable—it is extraordinary—as we achieve goals and continuously rise from one level of the social order to the next. The changes of attitude, behavior, mindset, relationships, and outlook on the world that occur in us are equally significant. That is why, with the exception of reminiscing about childhood or talking about sports, a purposeful, high-achieving professional will have little conversation in common with high school classmates, cousins, and neighborhood chums from back home whose iron has not been sharpened by the hot flame of rigor and true achievement.

> As iron sharpens iron, so one person sharpens another.
>
> —*Proverbs 27:17*

In addition, self-made high-achievers carry the heavy burdens and blessings that come along with success—making everything that they have achieved work in sync: power, wealth, leadership, responsibility, scrutiny, resilience. Nearly all self-made high-achievers have paid their dues and understand the loneliness that often accompanies their rise to the top. The air in which they fly is rare. The high-achiever knows that unless blessings are carefully managed, they may go much more quickly than they came. If not properly cared for, the house that they took years, sometimes decades, to build may burn to the ground overnight.

If others do not understand your place as you rise in the world order, use that to your advantage. Let it motivate you if you get discouraged on your journey to success. I challenge you to look at the sacrifices these people have made and the plan that they executed. *Did they have a plan? Did they execute it? Did they do anything other than accept the social order into which they were born?*

Whatever one's level of accomplishment, I admire and applaud equally the person who went from the underclass to working class, or from working class to middle class, or from middle class to upper-middle class, or from upper-middle class and so on. True class changes are more than just a job change or a swap in neighborhoods or cars. True class change represents a new world order for a person; a new way of thinking; a life-altering event; a rearrangement of friendships, relationships, thought processes, and subconscious.

Very rarely does a job, in and of itself, represent class. I know many people who lack income-earning power yet are in classes above where their income says they should land. For all who are on the rise or have achieved a rise in class, I respect that they saw more in themselves and were at least thirsty and uncomfortable enough to make the move to a higher station. I know that their climb was not easy. I salute them.

As I mentioned with Teddy, there is everything wonderful and right with being working class or middle class if that is the appropriate station to which you fully agree the universe has called you. And even though it appears that the rich are getting richer and the poor are getting poorer, working- and middle-class folks who feel stuck have a tool in their hands to effect change right now by applying the rules of this book. So when I talk about class changes, I do not speak to put down one class or another. Each one is filled with its own challenges. I write to talk about where you see yourself appropriately belonging and what you are capable of achieving. To see the light for the place where you belong, unlike Teddy, you must recognize and acknowledge your fear of going there, and then do something about it.

There is nothing wrong with success. Some people believe that many rich people have earned their money by hurting others, cheating the system, not playing fair, or playing a part in some other conspiracy theory. That's wrong, and just as happens with race, social classes need to stop pointing the finger at each other.

The rich people I know (and whom I choose to include in my life) have earned their money by doing right by the world and working for it. The door of success is open to all who put their fears aside and dare to knock. The cage in which you believe people have placed you is never as frightening as the cage in which you have already placed yourself. What cage have you created for yourself and trapped yourself in? Finding the key to unlock your cage is easy. Just begin with liberating your mind and changing your thoughts. Think positive thoughts daily about yourself. Love yourself. Inhale goodness and exhale your gold to the world. Breathe. Brainwash yourself in positivity and self-encouragement. Of all the things that you do, be willing to live like no one else will for a few years so that you can live like no one else can for the rest of your life. You will be glad you did.

PURPOSEFUL MILLIONAIRE POWER PLAY

1. Recognizing, nurturing, building, and expanding upon the gift or talent that the universe has blessed you with is, in my opinion, the highest and most honorable goal in life. Some people never find their gift, and worse yet, many people are told to silence or bury their gift. What is it that you are skilled and natural at doing that you love more than anything else in the world? For example, when I am speaking in front of an audience, I am in my absolute glory,

and it is my gift to the world. The time flies by, and I relish every second of it. What is your true gift, your gift that you were born to do and share with the world? What have you been doing to develop this gift and bring it into the lives of others? Is your day job in conflict with your true gift? If so, you must find a pathway to execute your gift so that the universe can receive more of the true you.

2. Now that you have identified your gift, reflect on whether your current environment is allowing you to develop that gift. Do you have loved ones or friends who criticize your dreams to develop your gift? Being around loved ones can bring some degree of comfort and familiarity, but if loved ones are not supportive of your dreams, they can be horribly debilitating. Is your home life, community, or town in which you live incapable of embracing your gift? If these things are true, reflect upon the words "get the hell out" and what they could mean to your future. Write down what you will do to change your environment so that your gift may flourish. Put a specific date on when you will make a move.

3. Repeat out loud five times, "I have everything that it takes to be healthy, wealthy, and happy. I am a Purposeful Millionaire."

CHAPTER THIRTEEN

CHANGE YOUR NET-WORK TO CHANGE YOUR NET-WORTH

Find a group of people who challenge and inspire you, spend a lot of time with them, and it will change your life.

—Amy Poehler

ONE OF THE greatest challenges of being a first-generation high-achiever is that there is rarely ever a pre-existing network of successful people with whom to associate, who might assist you, and who might guide you on your climb. Your universe, good or bad, is generally limited to the surroundings in which you were raised. When we are from the circles of our youth deprived of surgeons, judges, scientists, political leaders, academicians, and CEOs with whom to associate, from whom we might learn, and by whom we might be mentored, we are deprived of relevant role models. If we cannot see what we can be, how can we aspire to be it? Role models are few and far between and often relegated to fictional people on TV, some of whom may look like you, or not.

If in a place like the southern foothills of Virginia there are few models for professional success and even fewer for financial success, then a harsh reality of the world in which we live is that social class cycles almost invariably perpetuate. Here is the truth that most folks are not willing to admit publicly: working-class folks tend to raise children who grow up to be working class. Middle-class folks tend to raise children who grow up to be middle class. Rich folks tend to raise children who grow up to be rich folks, and they remain that way if their parents can train them to avoid squander and self-destruction sometimes prompted by the trappings of privilege, youthful boredom, or lack of appreciation. As sad as it is to say, these rules about class perpetuation hold pretty darn true. Success breeds success, lack of success breeds lack of success, dysfunction breeds dysfunction. People are truly a chip off the old block. What are you doing to journey to another block?

These paradoxes exist in our society that prides itself on every person's ability to achieve the American Dream if he or she works hard enough. This belief is both true and untrue. Hard work can get you very far in America. However, hard work without strategy will not get you very far unless you have some meaningful direction from at least one or two folks who have personally achieved at the level to which you aspire, who can help you avoid pitfalls along your journey. These folks are your network, your role models, your associates, and your clients. Rock-solid relationships with them play a major role in where your life will go.

Rule #37: Change Your Net-Work to Change Your Net-Worth: Always be busy expanding your network.

As a person on the pathway to higher achievement, make your trajectory easier by changing your net-work, which will in due time change your net-worth. Old friends are fine, and they have their place in your life and play an important role in your social support. However, new friends and a strong network of high-achieving peers who respect your work ethic and vision will bring you more professional referrals and dollars than you ever imagined.

On your journey to your dream, because these new friends are critical to your future success, spend more time with them; talk with them; ask questions; and discuss best practices about life, productivity, wealth creation, and career goals. Also, get to know them on a personal level as well—it is not always about business. Conversations about personal matters establish trust and open the doors for deeper conversations about business and financial affairs. So as you rise, understand that your network is also constantly rising and maturing and that these relationships are symbiotic. As those around you become more successful, you will in turn become more successful. A rising tide in your trusted network will raise all ships.

Just as money compounds in an investment account, so do the benefits of solid professional networks. Throughout his illustrious career, the famous author and motivator Jim Rohn proclaimed again and again that our income is usually the average of the five people with whom we spend the most time. Nothing could be more true. For me, I believe that it is not only one's income that is the average of those five people, but also attitude, outlook on the world, positivity, discipline, and value systems.

Be careful with whom you spend time. Strive to lift yourself up by being around people who have achieved more than you— who have mastered things that you have not—so that you may learn from them and apply those lessons to your life. Do the work, and watch your network work for you. Relationships are a critical investment. Approach them with sincerity, and nurture them. They will ultimately benefit you.

As your business network develops, always be seeking new connections—new relationships that will open up the doors of opportunity. There is no gamesmanship or disingenuousness here: expanding your meaningful relationships is the reality of how the business world works. At no given three-month stretch of time should you not have met and found a way to stay in contact with at least ten new individuals who were not previously in your life. If after every three-, six-, and twelve-month period, you look back on your life and see yourself hanging with the same five or ten people, then your personal plan for advancement is fundamentally flawed. No exceptions. Sounds hard, right? Well it is.

Meeting new people is a lot of work. Nurturing relationships is a lot of work. But you must be willing to show up and do that work. This is a numbers game as well as a quality game. Become a master of your professional craft and create a network of as many self-made wealthy people as you can, and you will see doors beginning to open for you. These people have done the work to achieve their success and overcome countless obstacles, and having them on your speed dial will be one of your greatest investments.

> The richest people in the world look for building a network; everyone else looks for work.
>
> —*Robert Kiyosaki*

Changing your network is not always as simple as showing up at a new cocktail party or networking happy hour, or setting up a LinkedIn or Facebook account. Sometimes a new network comes from places that others may not immediately understand as critical to your expansion plan. For example, a few years ago, I moved into a dream home on a bluff on an exquisite street. Some of my neighbors are doctors and lawyers; however, most of them are entrepreneurs and successful businessmen and businesswomen. Many of them are self-made millionaires. Because my neighbors and I have gotten to know one another as well as one another's line of business, we have referred countless business opportunities to one another. In fact, because of these referrals and the trust that my neighbors have in me, it would be much more expensive for me to move out of the neighborhood than to stay.

Well, James, how does that work? The average person might think the home is nothing more than a large box on a nice parcel of land with a great view. To my neighbors and others who understand the level of accomplishment that is required to earn and maintain it, the home is nothing short of a *qualifier for success*. My neighbors rightfully believe that the owners of such properties have done something, if not many things, right in their lives. In essence, such a property requires the head of its household to be accustomed to wearing some serious big boy drawers to earn, maintain, staff, and run the place. Such property owners understand that their similarly-situated environments can be a vehicle for starting conversations, fostering business relations, and growing a professional network.

Last year, my firm was working on selling a line of business within our company portfolio that was related to an environmental technology interest to which one of my neighbors is deeply committed. In fact, his private equity family office is committed to various causes in environmental and conservation technology, and he is globally connected in this industry. When we had finally prepared the company for sale, including creating due diligence binders galore and going through several rounds of meetings with our lawyers, I took him to lunch.

One lunch meeting resulted in his reaching out to several of his most trusted partners in private equity to meet with me. Those meetings led to deeper discussions about whether this line of business we were selling would be a good fit for their private equity group's portfolio. Though the private equity group would ultimately determine that such a purchase was not a perfect fit for them, I met several new business contacts and friends throughout the process. These people made additional introductions that would ultimately help me to expand our line of business, which created significant value for the company and will eventually lead to our selling it for a price much higher than we anticipated. Though in the short term we did not have an immediate sale, I met some great people through the process who aided me in my long-term wealth game to potentially sell our line of business at a much higher sales price. You see, my net-*work* is increasing my net-*worth*.

Earlier in this book, we discussed how critical it is to be in the right environment to achieve our dreams. I want to revisit that fact and try not to beat a dead horse. My home is an example of the right environment. It signifies a certain level of success about me, *and* the physical proximity to business people as neighbors makes the home and neighborhood useful. I am the one, however, who is taking action by acting upon those circumstances. Anyone can sit in a big house and not reach out to neighbors. The average person would be satisfied running through its hallways, lying by the pool, and keeping to him or herself. But I know that that is *not* how business or life works. Tools are all around us for expanding our network: we just have to be willing to put ourselves out there and to get out of our boxes. The home did not create the business deals for me. I did. I used it as one of many tools in my chest.

What tools to expand your network might you be overlooking? Identify those tools and potential relationships that may be right in your own backyard which you may be overlooking. Have no fear in reaching out to others—people love to talk. Have a conversation. It costs nothing. Do not ever forget that. Once you come out of your shell and nurture greater relationships, the universe will begin to open doors for you and will rise up to provide for you at the level at which you dream. Expand your net-work and your net-worth will inevitably follow.

Rule #38: Always Show Up.

I want to be very clear about this rule: often the hardest part of networking is showing up. For the most part, people do not show up (and they certainly do not follow up). They say that they will attend something and plan to attend, but life, or perhaps lack of confidence, kicks in. The little saboteur on their shoulder tells them that it is better to stay hunched over at their computer in their office or in the confines and serenity of the home. Nothing discouraging or insulting to the ego can take place in those comfortable, private places, right? There is no social awkwardness there. Showing up takes guts. To expand your network, you have to show up.

Perhaps this fear of showing up comes from subconscious thoughts of potentially being rejected because such people are introverts or because someone might not laugh at their joke, or whatever. Let me be honest: I am half introvert-half extrovert. My personality is pretty much a balance of both. Call me an "ambivert" whose natural tendencies are to enjoy a crowd from time to time but at other times to be at home reading a book instead of being inflicted by the pain of injecting myself into a crowd of people whom I do not know. Luckily, I know that the introvert side of me is a serious weakness when it comes to working on improving my net-work, which fuels my net-worth. I do my best to overcome that weakness by showing up.

One of the best client opportunities that ever came my way happened because I was in the right place at the right time. Earlier that day, I had a conversation with myself: "James, you have a lot of work to do, and you are tired. You should just go home and enjoy a glass of wine tonight and fall asleep."

That day, I had to battle my own internal reluctance to attend a networking reception being hosted by an old client. I almost never get headaches, but I had certainly created one for myself stewing over the option to attend or not. I was tired and had pondered every reason not to show up. So, instead of giving in to the forces of laziness and my natural introvert-like tendencies, I gave myself a pep talk: "James, you must show up. Just walk into the room and start talking to people. If you do not like the event, then leave. But you must first show up. You will never know what could have happened if you do not make the effort to show up."

That evening, I did show up. I walked into the room and was surprised to see three or four faces that I knew. Within minutes, an old friend introduced me to his associate, and she talked with me about an urgent consulting need that her Fortune 500 company had. That one conversation led to a seven-figure account for Excel Global Partners. I showed up, and my firm reaped the benefits. Cha-ching!

Rule #39: Understand the Know,
Like, Trust formula.

Life is not a popularity contest. Popularity contests usually don't focus on quality, just numbers. I have known quite a few people of less than adequate substance or character, but who happen to be quite popular. Being popular does not work for me; being respected does. To the contrary, life (and business as well) is a quantity *and* quality contest. The more successful, self-made, wealthy, and other high-quality people you know, the more likely it is that a lucky lightning strike will hit you when opportunity arises within your network. Without quality relationships, there will be little opportunity for advancement. The formula for genuine relationships looks like this:

Know + Like + Trust = Relationship

Networking is a two-way street. For example, I joyfully send referrals to people whom I have come to know, like, *and* trust. If they do not, however, meet my three-pronged test, they will not receive a referral from me. The same is true from those who know me. I fully accept that people may know or trust me but may not like me. They might not like something about my personality, the way I speak or dress, or something about how I carry myself may rub them the wrong way. That's human nature, and I am completely cool with that. I not only accept that fact but also understand the rules of the game and don't waste time forcing myself upon people who don't wish to get to know me, especially when there are literally billions of other people in the world with whom I could be spending time. I have options when it comes to relationships—lots of them—and you do too.

As we dig deeper into the *Know, Like, and Trust* test, understand that the test is particularly useful in environments that foster wealth creation. Folks who are at the highest levels of success tend to live in the same area, be members of the same overlapping clubs, and support similar overlapping charitable organizations. By flocking in the same areas, they get to see one another frequently and get to know one another: their habits, rituals, disciplines, good qualities, and shortcomings. This exposure provides them with the opportunity to get to know, like, and trust one another—or to know, dislike, and distrust one another.

Truthfully, communities of successful people are not perfect—they are microcosms of the greater world. As in every other place, there are some folks who talk about each other like dogs. They gossip about one another and pick apart one another's flaws. They are humans. The same is true in other types of places, such as in my hometown of Lynchburg where I learned and accepted this early on in life. Because you cannot force people to like and trust you, follow this advice: always keep your reputation as clean as possible because communities of success can be just as gossipy and petty as small towns. Always do the right thing because people will find out about the wrong thing a hundred times faster than all the right things you do. People love to gossip so guard your reputation like a fortress. Trying to repair it is usually a great deal harder than being constantly disciplined to keep it clean.

Frequently crossing paths on common turf, upper-crust people have constructive conversations among their insular circles about their children and schools, and also about world affairs, wine, golf, tennis, charity, skiing, yachting, theater, upcoming fundraisers, and so on. As cruel as it may sound, there is a language of success that is shared among them, and people who know that language fit in; those who do not are politely rejected or ignored (or worse yet, cause eyes to roll). The most successful individuals know that they must look the part and that every opportunity may be an opportunity for business. Even at the grocery store, they know that looking the part is critical to respect—that is, being known, liked, and trusted. They know that luck strikes at any given moment, so flip-flops and tank tops are not to be worn in public but rather in the privacy of their own home. On more than one occasion, I have been stopped in the grocery store or at the gas station to discuss business. I had the incumbent fluency to talk business with these individuals, and they knew me, liked me, and trusted me enough to be considered a resource for their issue. At the time, I most certainly was not wearing flip-flops or sporting what some folks would call a "wife-beater."

In the event that I make a referral and, on the rare occasion, my friend fails to deliver, my reputation may suffer damage. The damage could be irreparable. That's why it is always important to proceed with caution, guard your reputation like a fortress, and make smart decisions grounded in fact, not emotion. You get one reputation. Protect and do the work that is needed to always manifest a rock-solid value system.

Rule #40: Happy, lucky people surround themselves with happy, lucky people. Restrict your time with unhappy, unlucky people, including certain family and friends.

By severely restricting your time with unlucky, unhappy, downtrodden, or small-minded people, you begin to develop a wonderfully clear and positive mindset. That clear mindset is not muddled by the presence of miseducation, misfortune, regrets, and small thinking, all of which are grounded in emotion rather than facts. Because they are stuck muddling through their counterproductive emotions, such people have no power to determine their destinies. Negative emotions close doors; they shoo away any opportunity for achievement.

Winners think like winners, and they are fun to be around. Unlucky people have stinky attitudes, and the misery of their clouded universe is woefully contagious. Perhaps you have a few family members like this whom you need to begin avoiding, or maybe some friends whose only *modus operandi* is to drag you down with them. Avoid them, don't take their calls or respond to their text messages, and make any excuse necessary not to be in their presence. They will steal your mojo, wrap their problems and misfortune around your spirit, and squeeze the joy and purposefulness out of your life. If need be, you can even tell them that you are headed in a different direction in your life and need to spend more time around positive people who will lift you up. It takes guts to say that to folks. It takes even more guts to do it and stay focused on executing your plan.

> Respect yourself enough to walk away from anything that no longer serves you, grows you, or makes you happy.
>
> —*Robert Tew*

When happy, lucky people fall short in life or accidently stub their toe on the coffee table, they don't curse the universe, seek to blame someone else, or vacuum the positive energy out of others by cursing and bellyaching; they merely shake it off and keep moving forward. Be a happy, lucky person by working on constantly developing and surrounding yourself with a network of happy, lucky, like-minded businesspeople. It's that simple.

PURPOSEFUL MILLIONAIRE POWER PLAY

1. Happy, lucky people surround themselves with happy, lucky people. The people with whom you spend the most time are the people whom you are most like. Take five minutes to write down the names of the five people in your social or business network with whom you spend the most time and rank their general attitude on a scale of 1-10 (1 being the worst negative attitude possible, and 10 being the brightest, most positive attitude). Be honest with yourself as you do this exercise because as you evaluate the attitudes and moods of others, you are getting a clearer snapshot of yourself.

    a. Name: _____;
        General Attitude: _____

    b. Name: _____;
        General Attitude: _____

    c. Name: _____;
        General Attitude: _____

    d. Name: _____;
        General Attitude: _____

    e. Name: _____;
        General Attitude: _____

    Now look at the variance in the scores of the five different people. Who has the lowest score? Does that person promote your dreams or crush them? Who has the highest score? Does that person promote your dreams or crush them? Which person do you enjoy being around the most? Commit to surrounding yourself with more people like this person.

Now calculate the average score of the general attitudes by adding them all together and dividing them by 5. What is the average score? If the average of those attitudes or moods is closer to a 1 than to a 10, you need to work on developing a whole new network.

Finally, look at the individual scores for attitude and determine the one or more people whom you will spend significantly less time with in your life. If someone generally has a crabby attitude, then why the heck are you investing your precious time in that person? Make a change for Pete's sake!

2. Take a moment to think about three people within your social circle whom you do not know personally but whom you admire because of their achievements and success. Within the next week, ask other people in your network to make an introduction to them. If you cannot get anyone to make an introduction to them, directly invite your target to lunch, or at a minimum, ask your target for a ten-minute phone call if they are super busy (which they most likely are). When you meet, pick their brains for nuggets of wisdom regarding financial achievement and ask them about their story and how they got to where they are. Open up to them, be vulnerable, and share your financial and life goals. Ask them for advice, stay in contact with them, and always thank them for their time. Most likely, they will be glad to share encouraging words, offer advice, and stay in contact

with you. People love to talk about themselves, so ask good questions, and take notes!

3. Repeat out loud five times, "I have everything that it takes to be healthy, wealthy, and happy. I am a Purposeful Millionaire."

CHAPTER FOURTEEN

COMPOUND YOUR TALENT AND MONEY

EVERYONE WANTS MONEY. Don't let anyone fool you into thinking otherwise. Other than love, money is the greatest and most powerful currency on earth. Most people also want some kind of talent. It distinguishes one person from the next, the good from the great. However, neither money nor talent is mystical. Both are attainable through discipline. You just have to be willing to do the work.

So long as you are consistently disciplined with managing and growing your cash and your talent, both will increase significantly over time. Let's talk about how you must first work for your money and your talent, but with discipline, your money and your talent begin to work for you. This is what is called the compounding effect.

Compounding can be defined as the process of generating earnings on an asset's reinvested earnings. When the laws of compounding are understood, respected, and applied, a dollar can be multiplied over time, and a talent can be expanded beyond one's greatest imagination. In effect, because of the compounding effect, money and talent multiply.

Because most people are not willing to lay the initial foundation by taking the first step and committing to something by practicing, developing, and executing it over the long haul, they are not able to tap into the tremendous benefits of compounding. When I say "executing it over the long haul," I am not talking about a six-week, six-month, or three-year endeavor. I am talking about serious dedication over a significant course of time (sometimes ten or twenty years, or even a lifetime) with a consistent discipline to increasing one's universe.

TALENT

I am convinced that every man, woman, and child walking this earth is blessed with a certain talent. That talent can range tremendously across people, but the bottom line is clear: there is no one who is void of a special gift. That's why I love getting to know people: it is fun to learn about the uniqueness of others. A person's special talent or gift may range from being naturally comical to being blessed with exceptional athletic prowess. That gift could also manifest in the form of a talent with mathematics, science, people skills, or the arts. Everyone has a gift though some folks bury their talent or never do the work to uncover it. Some folks have more than one talent, but everybody has at least one.

Rule #41: Discipline is the key to advancing talent. Without discipline, talent will never develop or create sustainable success.

What distinguishes those who succeed and make something of their talent is discipline. For example, though it may look easy because of her years of training, Adele (or insert your favorite diva's name here) does not just walk onstage and belt out a tune that brings tears to your eyes. Her amazing voice, which first started as a God-given gift, had to be built upon, studied, refined, and improved over the years with voice lessons, countless hours in the studio, and care and attention to the overall health of her vocal chords. For Adele, the discipline of her talent allows her to be the respected star that she is. She is not a symbol of luck or good fortune; she is a symbol of hard work in disguise.

The ability to be Adele, Beyoncé, or Aretha Franklin, a self-made multimillionaire, or a world-renown surgeon is the result of thousands and thousands of hours of work that many others were simply unwilling to do. While Adele was on her rise, ordinary aspiring singers were trying to take the quick karaoke elevator up to success. But one thing I know for sure is that success is not easy and that the difference between successful and unsuccessful people is that successful people are willing to do lots of things that they do not want to do to get to the top, including locking themselves in a studio or office for countless hours until results are achieved.

Certainly, for successful people, there was some element of luck involved, which may have included being in the right place at the right time. However, I can name just as many great singers and businesspeople who were initially disciplined in advancing their careers but who ultimately crashed because they lacked the discipline to manage that success once it was achieved. They ended up jobless, divorced (again and again), homeless, on drugs, or worse, dead.

It takes discipline to hold success together and to build upon it. To the chagrin of custodians who mismanage success that falls into their laps by luck, they fail to realize that success that is worked for and sustained is the greatest of all drugs, analgesics, aphrodisiacs, or happy pills. Success is my drug of choice and has made me feel better than anything that I have ever consumed into my body; therefore, with discipline, I maintain it and grow my talents. As my talent compounds, my success compounds ever so beautifully. Now that's nirvana!

Rule #42: Increase your talent in a compounding fashion, just as you increase your financial assets.

Malcolm Gladwell handily illustrates the power of compounding in his book *The Tipping Point*. He illustrates that once we reach ten thousand hours of experience or practice in our talent, we reach a point of skill and experience that naturally results in greater opportunity and advancement. Just like a house of cards whose tipping point is reached, opportunity falls readily into the hands of the disciplined individual.

In today's world of social media and reality television, it is clear that many people are not willing to do the work to achieve their dreams. Society is filled with talentless overnight stars whose greatest achievement is a leaked sex tape or a proclivity to curse or gossip. Just think about how popular those "Housewives" shows are, or anything related to the Kardashian clan. Vanity, love of being in front of the cameras, and bad manners are not true talent. Television and social media cause young people to be confused about what success at its core really is. In addition, when fame or money is achieved without due work, both will eventually be fleeting.

Unlike the Housewives or the Kardashians, self-made people who are *true* success stories are wise. They earn their reputation and dollars each day, discipline themselves so that they can develop themselves, and allow the power of compounding to increase their prosperity. New opportunities for advancement are attracted to them because of their discipline and attitude. They create, respect, and maintain a life of sustainable abundance through the power of compounding their talents, which unlike reality TV stardom, can never be taken away from them.

I have greater respect for people who are truly self-made success stories, regardless of their level of fame or financial accomplishment, than for anyone else in this world. Following a mode of life similar to our formula of **Idea + Plan + Execution = Success**, self-made people came up with their idea of success, created a plan to achieve it, and executed that plan. Starting from nothing and ending up with great success is the embodiment of the American Dream. Certainly, some people started with less than others, but even many who were advantaged did little with their talent and thus turned out to be just another Joe. This is shameful in my opinion.

For me, cultivating my talents every day and witnessing the outcome of their compounding is a form of worship. This steadfastness in execution is a way for me to manifest gratitude to the universe for blessing me with opportunity. Work frees my mind and body to deliver upon the very purposes for which I was born. By doing the work and walking closer toward my dreams each day, I am making manifest the power of the universe and living up to the potential that God has given me.

Not living up to my potential would be my greatest failure. It would cause me shame and disappointment with myself. So, I will continue climbing the stairs. And besides, each step gets easier to climb because my talent, and thus capability to handle more challenges and responsibility, is compounding ever so beautifully.

Rule #43: Use routine and daily habits to keep chipping away at your dreams. You will eventually create a beautiful sculpture.

Each day—weekday, weekend, or holiday—I rise and go to bed at the same time. I rise at roughly 5:30 a.m. and lie down to rest at roughly 10 p.m. This disciplined schedule puts my mind, body, and spirit into a rhythm of purposefulness each day. On the weekends, there is usually no sleeping in. It throws me off. Lying in bed pulls me away from achieving my goals and goals certainly don't go into hibernation on the weekends. Once I have gotten enough restorative rest, it's time to get moving so that I can hit my morning rituals, get some work done, and continue chipping away at my dreams.

Every morning when I wake, I make a cup of coffee and then do twenty or so minutes of yoga and bodyweight exercises. I then immediately head to the library in my home to write. The writing can range from that of an article, a proposal, a chapter in a book, or something in my daily journal. Does that sound boring or monotonous to you? Not to me—this is my absolute favorite part of the day. Let me tell you why.

I believe that monotony and good habits can be tremendously advantageous. I get to jump out of bed each morning with excitement because I know that I will be applying and growing my talent, which in turn increases my universe. My increased universe leads to greater opportunity, which means more blessings. Pretty cool now, huh? Because of this attitude and approach, my work does not even feel like work, and because of that, I would be hard-pressed to deviate from this schedule.

My morning writing goal is about 1,000 words before I move on to responding to e-mails and business affairs. Because I write roughly the same amount every day, I am able to produce approximately 365,000 words of writing each year. Though a significant amount of this writing is for professional purposes, some of it is creative. *The Purposeful Millionaire* is the result of writing at the same time each day with my goal of crafting something meaningful for others to learn. This book is in some ways my offering to the universe.

> We are what we repeatedly do. Excellence, then, is not an act but a habit.
>
> —*Aristotle*

Let's take a look at what 365,000 words of writing looks like in terms of printed material.

Depending upon a number of factors, a book of 200 pages is on average about 55,000 words. By writing roughly 365,000 words a year, I am able to produce the equivalent of about 6.5 books (of course, unedited, unmarketed, and unpublished—and editing, marketing, and publishing take up a ton of time, but bear with me; I am trying to make a point) of two hundred pages apiece! Now that's a lot of writing.

To the average person who does not understand the many purposes of discipline or the power of compounding talent, that would seem like a tremendous ordeal, perhaps even an impossible or insufferable amount of writing. To me, it seems like joy and because of the compounding effect, each day I write, I become a better and more efficient author. In pursuing my idea and executing my plan, I am able to create a significant amount of printed material, appear in publications, and not sweat the process of waiting for some kind of creative force to move me to produce the material. This is called discipline. Remember how the formula works:

Idea + Plan + Execution (<u>the hard part</u>) = Success!

I not only write but also read and do research each day. The materials that I read provide me with the knowledge base that I need to discuss complex affairs with other high-achievers on topics such as business, money management, political affairs, world events, and more.

On my worst day, I read approximately 5,000 words of literature that is related to my areas of expertise (management consulting, leadership, business strategy), and on my best day (often a whole Sunday outside loafing by the pool with my cellphone turned off), I have caught myself reading 100,000 words or more. My daily average is about 10,000 words. Each day, I carve out time to read, which ensures that I am as informed as possible and can apply best practices to the most important things in my life.

> The difference between where you are today and where you'll be in five years from now will be found in the quality of books you've read.
>
> —*Jim Rohn*

Now it is impossible for me to read all periodicals and to be apprised of everything that is happening in the world. However, by reviewing my go-to daily periodicals on business and world affairs, I can hold my own in conversations with other individuals of power and influence. If I were uninformed, misinformed, or ignorant of these things, then I would be taken as ignorant. I am able to speak with command and fluency through the language of knowledge—not opinions but fact-based knowledge. Just as iron sharpens iron, one person sharpens another.

Being able to speak intelligently about a relatively wide range of topics is not happenstance; it is the natural outcome of the discipline by which I have chosen to live. Because of these disciplines, or should I say habits, doors have opened for me because someone found me interesting, smart, well-informed, or all of the above. The daily reading average of 10,000 words over the course of one year results in a total of about 3,650,000 words or the equivalent of about sixty 200-page books! The library and bookshelves in my house are evidence of this, along with my recycle bin full of periodicals. Even if my brain retains only a small percentage of the information in those readings, that's a lot of knowledge gained that I would not have otherwise had if I had parked myself in front of a television and watched reality TV!

> What you do every day is more important than what
> you do once in a while.
>
> *–Gretchen Rubin*

Another wonderful example of the compounding effect is how it can apply to our physical health and spirituality. To live a fully actualized, happy life, I am dedicated to both. Each day, regardless of where I find myself in the world, after I rise in the morning, I commit to at least twenty or so minutes of weight lifting and/or yoga—both of which I use to meditate on the universe's beauty, or in other words, to quiet my mind from business and personal affairs. This routine feeds me both physically and spiritually.

Now this may not sound like a lot that I am committing to this physical and spiritual practice, and you may be thinking, "Well, when I go to the gym, I bust it out for two hours straight, and James is obviously not working out as hard as I do!" My response is, "Good for you. Do you consistently go to the gym for two hours straight, and are your workouts effective?" Allow me to explain in greater detail how my relatively easy twenty-minute daily discipline works and has brought great benefit to my well-being.

Rule #44: To achieve goals, make sure
that they are specific, measurable,
attainable, relevant, and time-bound.

In his interview of John Lee Dumas of the podcast *Entrepreneur On Fire* regarding Dumas' book, *The Freedom Journal*, Jon Nastor writes about the power of setting attainable goals. In *The Freedom*

Journal, Dumas illustrates how we can take vague goals and turn them into true achievements. Here is how he defines a S.M.A.R.T. goal:

- **Specific:** Clearly defined goals get accomplished; vague hopes become forgotten.

- **Measurable:** The goals should be able to be tracked qualitatively and quantitatively.

- **Attainable:** Think big, but keep it achievable.

- **Relevant:** Set goals that further you, your business, and your purpose.

- **Time-bound:** Aim for a hundred days or fewer.

Putting this methodology to task, on an average day, I do approximately 50 pushups and 25 burpees in the morning as part of my focused physical exercise routine. Over the course of one year, this discipline results in at least 18,250 pushups and 9,125 burpees. Pretty cool, right? I don't even have to waste time driving across town to the gym because I know that I consistently force myself to knock out these exercises each day, the physical and mental benefits of which are so rewarding.

The benefit of having discipline is that my exercise routine and results exceed those of people who brag to me about going to the gym for two hours once, twice, maybe three times a month, if they are lucky, or the guy who "works out" for two hours and spends an hour of it playing on his smartphone. At their best, they have achieved an hour or two, or only a little more, of ineffective, unfocused time in the gym each month, while I have achieved no less than 600 minutes of focused, sweat-inducing, spiritually liberating workouts in the comfort and privacy of my hotel room or home each day.

Being in great integrity with our physical body and consistently taking excellent care of our health is a great part of the equation. So I keep my exercise routine uncomplicated, and thus it is highly sustainable. No gym at all is needed for me. No commute, no traffic, no worrying about sweaty laundry and towels, no time wasted socializing by the treadmill. No excuses. If I forget my workout clothes, I just do yoga or body weight exercises in my birthday suit, which keeps me completely aware of what is going on with my body, especially if I am putting on an unnecessary pound or two. My return on this easy investment of discipline and time is simply a solid, healthy body with lots of energy that helps me to keep up with the rigors of my schedule and travel demands. I am proud to take care of it as an act of appreciation to the universe for blessing me each day with good health. I live in complete acceptance, integrity, and appreciation for my body by adhering to my daily habit—a discipline that has become much easier, more routine, and more beneficial for me over time.

You will find many people who say that they do not have the time for mental and physical improvement. When someone tells me that, my natural reaction is to shudder. When I think about the rigor of consistently working sixty hours a week (sometimes many more, though my partner is known to rock an eighty-hour plus work week like a champ) and the days that I feel like not pushing myself as hard, or doing anything at all, I reflect on the power of compounding, and I do it anyway, even if for a shorter period. That is what winners do. If I were to ever move into the excuse mode and shun the execution mode, success would quickly slip from my hands.

Idea + Plan + Excuses = Failure

<u>AND</u>

Idea + Plan + Lack of Willpower = Failure

To give myself a frame of reference and to humble the heck out of me, I like to give myself a swift kick in the bum by comparing my schedule to, for example, that of former President Obama (who had many more responsibilities and headaches than I or anyone else on the planet had during his eight years in office). Because I have the privilege of being friends with a couple of people who worked closely with him, I understand the demands of his schedule. I also understand how the man committed time to taking care of his body every morning by exercising almost infallibly. I find this fact very interesting because a president is afforded much less free time than I, yet most successful presidents have managed to read just as much or more than I on a daily basis, meet with more people than I, and handle many more issues than I could possibly fathom. POTUS also has a tremendous staff to aid him, but even then, the nature and stresses of his global responsibilities should not be underestimated. Leading the free world is not easy. My life can be considered a cakewalk compared to that of any POTUS. I use that frame of reference to remind me how easy I have it when I find myself pouting or not wanting to leave the comfort of my warm bed in the morning.

Therefore, I will not complain. I will execute. I will dutifully keep chipping away at my plan, which I always remind myself is a giant block of ice that is slowly melting away with time, until my masterpiece sculpture is created. If someone were to complain to me about not having enough time, I would encourage him or her to watch less television (perhaps none at all, for that matter), to gossip less, and to get as organized as possible. It's that simple.

Speaking of television, the average American watches so much television that it is almost a full-time job! *The New York Times* reports that each day, Americans watch 5.4 hours of television.[1] In addition, if we look at the *total* amount of time that is consumed on various types of media on a daily basis, which includes watching TV, surfing the web on a computer, using an app on a phone, or listening to the radio mindlessly, the time wasted more than doubles. Yikes! This is more than a full work day. Yet many folks eagerly offer the excuse, "I don't have enough time," when it comes to daily disciplines. Time spent loafing around or making excuses is time that could be spent being productive. Again, my advice is to stop gossiping, turn off TMZ, read a book (particularly one that provides expertise on your area of professional focus), begin executing your dreams, and your life will be refreshed.

I never knew a man who was good at making excuses who was good at anything else.

—*Benjamin Franklin*

I am by no means perfect, but I am self-aware enough to know that the universe has blessed me with gifts that I will not misinterpret as burdens. I receive my gifts with gratitude and ask the universe to provide me with more, as I am willing to do the work to ensure that they are not squandered. One thing I know for sure about how this universe treats talent and discipline is that by doing the work consistently as a routine or a good habit, I will find that opportunity appears from many places without much additional effort. Do the initial work, stick with your disciplines, and watch compounding work in your life. You will gain the Midas touch indeed.

---

1   http://www.nytimes.com/2016/07/01/business/media/nielsen-survey-media-viewing.html?_r=0

MONEY

Similar to talent, money must be treated with great respect. As our greatest currency other than love, money used improperly vanishes quickly. Money used wisely multiplies. People without solid financial footing often confuse money with power and assume that wealthy people use money only to buy flashy toys. That is only partially true and certainly not true for all wealthy people. What the non-wealthy do not always know is that money is more powerful than any toy. It is a tool for gaining experiences, opportunities, access, and assets that further aid the wealthy in increasing their abundance. Experiences, opportunities, and assets compound with time. Toys usually do not–they fall apart.

Rule #45: Money is our greatest currency other than love. When properly understood and handled, it compounds. Make your money compound by gathering it, growing it, and seldomly disturbing it.

The wealthy people I know certainly buy things and lots of them; however, because of their wealth, the things that they buy are not expensive for them. Wealthy people see most things as liabilities, so if they buy a new car, they see it as something that will decrease the balance in their bank account, not increase it. Again, a car is not an asset, and a primary residence is not an asset either.

People who are committed to increasing their financial station are committed to buying things that are assets (property with a value that is able to meet or exceed debts), not liabilities (a debt or financial obligation). As you master this knowledge, remember not to get confused by comparing yourself or your purchases to anyone because a new toy such as a Rolls Royce can be considered cheap to a wealthy man who is constantly accumulating more money into his assets column (investments, real estate, equity in businesses, etc.) than into his liabilities column (cars, watercrafts, designer clothes, etc.). Don't let other people's toys get you down. You will be there soon enough. Just keep reading.

The liabilities that we mentioned are just icing on the cake for wealthy people who are smart. The toys come *after* their assets are producing passive (not requiring them to work for it) positive income at a certain level. The reverse formula can be true for some people who are not wealthy. The toys come *before* the assets (if they have any) are producing passive income at a certain level. Those folks buy things to attempt to *look* rich. They are far from it and are at risk of losing it all. The things that they buy, often on credit, exceed what their income is able to pay for. The most dangerous aspect of this is that their income is often from working a job (active), not from other resources like passive investments. So if they lose their job or get sick, they also lose their ability to pay for their toys that they bought on credit. Once they are unable to make payments on their toys, the bank takes them away. This is the catch-22 of building wealth. If you are serious about building great wealth, you cannot worry about having flashy toys on your way to the top. Focus on yourself. Live simply and continue putting more into your assets column than your liability column, and you will achieve the life you wish.

Now that we have toys (a.k.a. stupid material junk that strokes our fragile egos) out of the way, let's dive even deeper into wealth creation. The rich understand the power of compounding. Like a talent that improves over the years owing to discipline, money, when applied correctly, will grow with little to no effort on the part of its holder. For example, if you invest $100 per month each year for the next twenty years, you do not simply end up with $100 x 12 months x 20 years = $24,000. You end up with a whole lot more. Even if we compound the $100-per-month investment conservatively with an 8 percent rate of return and reinvest our returns, we end up with more than $58,902. Pretty awesome, right? By doing nothing more than maintaining the discipline to deposit money on a monthly basis and not touching it, you have made $34,902. This is what assets are all about. They make money for you. They do not take it away from you.

Again, talent, time, and money are all assets. The effects of compounding work only if you consistently maintain the discipline to develop them with respect and great care. Discipline requires patience, something that many people do not have or understand. Discipline also requires maturity, which is also something that many people do not have or understand. Discipline creates great things in life, including financial abundance, unforgettable experiences, incredible talent, and more consistent levels of stability and happiness. And above and beyond all those positive outcomes, doing extremely long hard challenges is good for the soul—when you are growing, you are glowing. What could be better than that?

An old friend of mine, who is a retired CEO, has a saying that I love: "Happiness is positive cash flow." He is a cheapskate, drives an eleven-year-old chocolate brown suburban with a broken sunroof, and has an out-of-this world asset pool of real estate, stock, and equity holdings. But he is also a multimillionaire many times over. Though I am not asking you to live quite as miserly as him, his words ring true.

Increasing one's station in life to a much higher level is not for the faint of heart but really is achievable. In this world, there are millions of people who live in free countries and toil long hours of countless work each day, but who lack the discipline to execute any type of strategy to unshackle themselves from an existence that is less than their full potential. They are lazy when it comes to self-development and self-uplift, preferring to march lock-step on the path of sub-standard existence, or mediocrity at best; often complaining along the way that the universe has not been better to them.

Simply by reading this book, you are not one of those people. By understanding the principles of success and achievement, the openness of the world to you regardless of what you look like in the mirror, and the knowledge that the mind is your greatest asset, you are on a different path that will empower you to honor the universe by bringing your very best to it. Your life and everything that it touches will be compounded. You will work for the universe, and it will work for you.

PURPOSEFUL MILLIONAIRE POWER PLAY

1. Read, review, and learn the following guidelines regarding how compounding works. These guidelines work the same for talent as they do for money. If you have trouble with willpower, i.e. committing to anything over an extended amount of time, print out these guidelines and place them somewhere prominent. Read them daily and the seeds of their words will be planted in your subconscious.

a. The whole concept of compounding is that you must sacrifice today to receive huge benefits in the future.

b. You do not have to be super rich or super talented for compounding interest to work for you.

c. Time is your friend, so start early.

d. Compounding interest can hurt you very badly if you stop contributing or withdraw.

e. If you were to invest $10,000 with compounding interest at a rate of 9 percent per annum, the rule of 72 demonstrates that it would take 72/9 = 8 years for the investment to be worth $20,000! The only thing you have to do is to make the initial deposit. Don't worry about the formula or math if that is not your strength. Just know that compounding works incredibly in your favor!

f. The more you put in, the more you get out.

g. Lots of very normal people have gotten wealthy by allowing compounding to work for them.

h. It all adds up faster than you think!

2. What does "Money is the greatest currency other than love" mean to you? Have you ever fought with anyone about money? How did it make you feel? Write one paragraph about the action you will take to prevent such fights in the future.

3. Remember the formulas that: **Idea + Plan + Excuses = Failure**. Also, **Idea + Plan + Lack of Willpower = Failure**. It's that simple. Folks talk about how busy they are, but most of them are either lazy, or at a

minimum, they are extremely inefficient at managing their lives (execution). The fact of the matter is that people have a lot more time than they think—the average American watches more than five hours of television each day. This is crazy!

For the next week, keep a watch, timer, or clock by your television and write down how many hours you watch television each day. After the week is complete, vow to decrease your TV watching by 50 percent. The week after that, decrease your TV watching by another 50 percent until you eventually no longer watch TV and are so busy focused on executing your goals that you do not even notice that TV is no longer part of your life. You will be in a better mood by eventually eliminating the "gossip box" from your life. If you already do not watch TV, apply this rule to another area of your life. Perhaps it is texting or playing video games, shopping, surfing the Internet, or gossiping that is taking too much time out of your life to achieve your goal. Whatever it is, work on eliminating your distractions and time-wasters.

4. Repeat out loud five times, "I have everything that it takes to be healthy, wealthy, and happy. I am a Purposeful Millionaire."

CHAPTER FIFTEEN

START AND END
YOUR DAY RIGHT

Each night, when I go to sleep, I die. And the next morning when I wake up, I am reborn.

—*Mahatma Gandhi*

IF YOU SPEND five minutes describing to me exactly how you start and end your day, I can tell you exactly how successful you are, or better yet, how successful you will ever become. Shocking, right? But it's the truth. How we start something and end something, especially our days, thoroughly affects our journey on the road to achievement.

The way you start your day determines everything. Start your day wrong, and everything else goes wrong. Also, the way you end your day determines how you will start the next day. This cycle of *rest, start, stop; rest, start, stop* cannot be compromised if you are to commit your life to achievement. Lots of people talk about how little sleep they get and how hard they work. Instead of talking that nonsense, I like to talk about how well rested I am and about how focused and efficient I am at achieving my goals.

Society seems to think it's cool that people do not get the rest that their bodies and minds require. It's almost like bragging rights to talk about how hard you work or how little sleep you get. Something is seriously wrong with that picture. If the mind is not rested, then productivity suffers. Efficiency and accuracy decrease, and mistakes are made. What I have learned as a businessman is that sometimes folks, including myself, are required to grind it out and crank out a very long workday or series of workdays in excess of twelve or fourteen hours; however, this is not sustainable in the long term. It will eventually make you crash and burn.

When you crash and burn, it takes a great deal of spunk to get back on your path to success—way too much spunk. The time it will take you to get back on the right path is greater than anything you could ever gain by working endless hours, to say nothing of your neglect of your body, spirit, family, or significant other. The main thing is to learn the rules in this chapter so that you can commit to taking better care of yourself so that you never crash and burn again. If you are already great at taking care of yourself, then for heaven's sake, skip this chapter. But if you are like most of us entrepreneurial high-achieving workaholics out there, keep on reading.

If you can consistently get eight—perhaps ten or twelve—*good* hours of work out of a person five or six days out of the week, then you have a great worker. But don't expect a whole lot more hours of peak productivity in the long term from that person or from yourself. Or at least don't expect that person to be at peak productivity or to be happy in the long term. That is not to say that people are lazy: that is to say that people are human. Humans get tired and worn out. They are not machines. And besides, even machines need down-time and maintenance.

If workers are not accomplishing their tasks in roughly eight, sometimes ten hours each day, then a good boss needs to revisit their workload, the resources provided for them to do their job, and the internal sustainability strategy of the business. The same case goes for the boss. Though good bosses carry certain stresses with them twenty-four hours a day that their workers may not, good bosses are at their best when they practice what they preach.

Rule #46: Learn how to relax. You are
in this game for the long haul.

Relaxation is important. I spend nearly all my time in three places that I absolutely love when I don't have to travel for business. You can find me in either Austin, southern California, or Maui—the sunniness and unique character of all three help to bring out the best in me. I do not like the snow or cold weather, and the rejuvenation, both professionally and personally, that I find in these places that I consider little home bases are priceless. These environments, each with its own beautiful attributes, make me a better business leader, spouse, family man, and visionary. The thought of writing this book popped into my mind after a beautiful afternoon hike in the mountains of Maui on the east side of the island near Hana.

On this particular occasion, I had gotten a wonderful night's sleep and restorative rest; had awoken later than normal that morning, at 6 a.m., and cranked through writing, physical exercise, e-mails, and phone calls; and had made several executive decisions all by 11 a.m. Hawaii time. Taking advantage of the five-hour time difference between the place in Hawaii and our office headquarters in Texas, as well as the six-hour time difference between our eastern-region practice group, I knew that my team would be deep in their workday and sending me meaningful questions and concerns that they had attempted to work through before reaching out to me for help.

The time difference forces them to be more self-sufficient and empowers them with more executive authority without my looking over their shoulder. I like this for them and I like it for me. It makes us all better. I appreciate and admire them. Their teamwork and commitment to the Excel Global Partners and EGP Family of Companies brand allow me to have avoided having a stroke or heart attack by now. We work well together. They keep me healthy, and I do the same for them, but it first begins with knowing how to rest and relax to be our personal best in our professional endeavors.

I have the greatest efficiency on the Maui schedule because my executive team, all based on the mainland, know that when I am there, they have a limited number of hours to get a response from me before their workday ends. This system works. My interruptions are minimized, and in the morning, I am in the zone cranking through tasks at my peak level of productivity. My workday is just a few hours long, and the time flies by. It is actually rather fun cranking through things at warp speed. Thanks to a good night's rest and not lollygagging around the office, I sometimes get more done in one short morning workday in Maui than I do in a full day on the mainland. I have taken this practice with me to California and Texas even though I cannot take advantage of the time zone differences as well in those places. But one thing this has taught me for sure is that the early bird always gets the worm.

I digress. To return to how the idea of writing this book popped into my mind, after pretty effortlessly getting through my work that day, I found that the gorgeous afternoon hike gave me some "me" time. It gave me time to nourish my body with much needed movement away from sitting at a desk, which in turn nourished my spirit and creative mind. The feel-good sensation of having accomplished a great deal that morning, along with the benefit of strenuous physical exercise, fresh air, and a renewed spirit, aligned the perfect circumstances for all those forces to work together to launch *The Purposeful Millionaire.*

That afternoon, I would go back home to write the first chapter of the book that would become a new mission for me—sharing the good news of prosperity and the availability of the American Dream to all. That is how I know that morning focus and rituals work. The genesis of my most important ideas, plans, and executions have all happened in the morning for me. And a great night's rest doesn't hurt either.

Rule #47: Make your entire day important and relevant to your mission. You will never regain that time. How you spend your evening hours is just as important as how you spend your morning hours.

In the evening hours, I have learned a few things as well: 1) Never have that extra glass of red wine (which is my favorite, and I admit that sometimes I think I "deserve" it after a long day of work or travel) because even though it is delicious, alcohol will rob you of good sleep, and 2) Always reflect upon what you have accomplished that day, and write down what your three goals are to accomplish tomorrow. Reflecting upon your day's accomplishments, even if the list is short, places the mind in a state of success, accomplishment, and gratitude. Writing down three goals for the next day focuses the mind and prepares it for another day of meaningful execution.

These two actions create a ritualistic state of positive energy associated with your work. They set the tone for the next day and the next day and so on. Writing down goals for the next day allows your mind to rest and not churn a "to-do" list while you are sleeping. Instead of dreaming about that task list you have on your desk and what you have *not* accomplished, you can put those thoughts aside and dream about pleasant things that do not relate to work. This is what I call restoration. When I sleep, I sleep. I don't dream about work. I dream about dreams. I wake up happy.

The average person throughout his or her life spends a total of 6.5 years daydreaming. I like to do my dreaming at night while I am asleep so that I am not dreaming during the day about what I could and should have done with my life. Dreaming and great sleep rejuvenate the creative spirit. No worry, no tossing and turning—just dreaming, restoration, and rejuvenation. Powerful stuff, right?

Mahatma Gandhi said something that I live by: "Each night, when I go to sleep, I die. And the next morning when I wake up, I am reborn." By allowing the worries of the day to die at night, the mind, body, and spirit are placed at rest. When your feet (or knees in prayer) hit the ground in the morning, you are born again—refreshed and ready for the next day with a new mind, body, and spirit. But you must choose to do this. Moreover, we start a new life each day; each day we have a new universe, a new dynamic with the universe, and a new opportunity to build upon our successes, or alternatively to correct any mistakes or trespasses from the previous day. Use this clean slate that you will be granted every waking day of your life to your advantage.

On another note, if you have any aches and pains, just like everyone else, you would be amazed at what this type of die-at-night deep restorative rest can do for your body along with purchasing a really high-quality memory foam or hybrid mattress and great sheets. All body aches and jokes aside, on days when I do not feel like getting out of bed, I roll (it's really more like a flop) out of bed and land on my knees. While on my knees, I say a prayer for strength to start my day. This always works. Then I get moving. The universe never fails to push me forward when I make the request.

All this rest and rejuvenation talk is for your own personal and professional benefit. Everything—and I mean everything—is tied to your ability to be the best that you can be, not just for yourself, but for others. The boss who is constantly working impossible hours and "cranking it out" is a "cranky" boss. He is the boss whom people do not enjoy working for. He is impatient. He is not a good teacher. He is not understanding. He is a poor listener and problem solver. And he is certainly not efficient or at the peak of his productivity.

Whenever I have made a bad decision or gotten short with someone, I can almost always go back and reflect upon how well I am taking care of myself or sleeping. I caught myself recently when I snapped at someone for a petty matter, apologized to the person, and immediately reflected upon my sleep patterns and wellness routine. I put a remediation plan in place for myself by making sure that I got my tail in the bed on time each night for the rest of the week. I put James first so that I could return to bringing my best—not my sleep-deprived worst—to the world.

By putting yourself first and caring for your mind, body, and spirit above all things, you will find that everyone around you benefits. The effect is truly trickle-down. Good leadership begins at the top and trickles down through any organization, including families. Bad leadership does the same thing.

If your home life or business affairs are a mess, maybe it is time that you did some work on yourself. If you take the time to dig deeply into each situation, you will see that you are either the root of all of your blessings, or you are the root of all of your problems.

Learn how to restore yourself, care for yourself, and do the work to be a great leader. Get some rest, and put yourself first. It will do your mind, body, and spirit plenty of good.

PURPOSEFUL MILLIONAIRE POWER PLAY

1. Have you ever wondered how some of the most powerful and wealthiest people in the world start their day? It is certainly not by hitting the snooze button or by trying to ail a hangover. The majority of billionaires wake up early in the morning and have daily routines that consist of mental exercises and meditations that they consider keys to their success. Many of them accomplish more by 9 a.m. than many people accomplish all day, or all week, for that matter... Are you a morning person or a night person? If you are a night person, you may be missing out on some of the most powerful, creative, and wonderful hours of your day. If you do not believe me, I challenge you to search the Internet by typing in the following: *why waking up early is healthier*. You will be overwhelmed with the information you find.

ACTION ITEM: For the next five days, set your alarm clock to wake you up thirty minutes earlier. Promise yourself that you will not hit the snooze button! Create a morning ritual that works for you, whether that be meditation, yoga, running, weight-lifting, or writing in your journal. Then you can turn to work. Whatever you do, take this time to care for yourself and your mind. Do not check e-mails, watch TV, or check the news. Set your smartphone in airplane mode.

This is time for you to invest in yourself to create discipline and rituals that will serve you in accomplishing more and creating a better and happier life for yourself. Learn to like waking up early, and enjoy the peaceful hours of the morning. For the following five days, set your alarm clock thirty minutes earlier and do it again and again until you feel that you have reached the optimal wake-up time for your mood and productivity.

2. Repeat out loud five times, "I have everything that it takes to be healthy, wealthy, and happy. I am a Purposeful Millionaire."

PART IV
THE SUCCESS

IDEA + PLAN + EXECUTION = *SUCCESS*

CHAPTER SIXTEEN

ENJOY THE RIDE

There are some things that money can make a lot worse. Money will never solve a mental problem or a money problem.

—*Iyanla Vanzant*

CONGRATULATIONS! THE DISCIPLINES that you have mastered have gotten you to the Success portion of your journey. Your discipline will help keep you here or prepare you to reach a higher level of success. Now that you have achieved your financial goals, all the work is done, right? Wrong! We have a long way to go. Success is its own journey. It is the beginning of a new phase of life that will challenge your previous thoughts, practices, and behaviors as well as test your ability to be flexible, resilient, and humble.

Just as with handling money, success must be cared for ever so delicately. Success is not just financial: it is emotional and spiritual—and it is not always static. Those who want the most out of the success phase put great care and time into mastering happiness. I remind you that happiness is a choice, and it is also a practice. Many people screw up success and happiness because they require a different kind of work and commitment that go above and beyond professional and financial pursuits. Sadly, many people never get a real taste of either success or happiness, let alone become masters of them because they are somewhat of an ever-moving target. Here's why: success has a snowball effect. The more of it you achieve, the more you will have an insatiable appetite for more. And it sure does taste yummy! Let's talk about how you can enjoy all of its deliciousness.

In the success phase, you will see people's character, as well as demons and flaws, come out more clearly than in any other phase of their journey. That is why I use a special analogy in this chapter to illustrate how your mindset will affect whether your success can be maintained and sustained or not. I want you to take this advice to heart: *what got you to this level is not what is going to keep you at this level, or take you to the next level. Your game must now change. Your mindset must now change.*

As a credit to you, your mindset is what got you to this stage and what determined how much you enjoyed your journey getting here. If you got through all of the stress of getting here without gaining some bad habits along the way, then double congratulations to you!

As you know, your mind is indeed the most powerful tool in the world—a tool for creating opportunity—and it can be disciplined and adjusted appropriately to avoid some of life's new challenges, which could lead to inescapable pitfalls. Keep in mind that money and success do not change a person; they merely reveal to the world who a person truly is. That is why this phase can be tricky for many people. I have known and personally witnessed folks "succeed" who were horribly flawed creatures but who made it to the success phase in spite of their shortcomings. The problem is that once they made it to the top, they did not address and remedy their flaws. One person, in particular, made it to a high political office only to be indicted in a fraud scheme that would land him in prison for more than a decade. Another made forty million dollars before he turned thirty-five years old and lost it all due to his obsession with the fast life of partying and womanizing. And yet another became so idly bored once he made it to the success stage, he lost his medical license and is barred from ever practicing again in his state. These tragic mishaps are exactly why I wrote this chapter. I want you to keep and grow all of what you have worked for and to find peace and long-term fulfillment at this stage—true sustainable wealth and happiness.

I use the analogy of people's driving habits and styles to further illustrate the power of the mind. This analogy is particularly relevant because it is quite possible for you to get to the success stage by exercising plenty of flaws (i.e. bad driving habits), but you will surely fall from that glorious pedestal if you do not find a way to fix or tame them. Recall that I mentioned earlier that the game that got you to the success level is absolutely *not* the game that will keep you at this level or take you to the next level. Your habits must change.

Knowing that bit of advice, take a moment to visualize cars traveling down a busy urban street, all driven by drivers with unique personalities and thus unique driving traits. Reflect on how the drivers' habits are basically a reflection of who they are at their core. All the drivers will eventually get to their desired destination, but many of them will do so with a certain amount of self-inflicted chaos or unnecessary drama. At the very special stage of great success, which is rarely achieved by others, there is no space for chaos, drama, flipping off others, or rule-breaking.

Skill, deep breaths, appreciation for the journey, and a steady hand are needed to sustain this phase. Let's take a look at some of these drivers who will need to change their ways to make this phase of their lives sustainable.

Speeders: Just as they might drive a car, some people have sped through their journey to success without ever having enjoyed the view. They rushed from one meeting to the next, signed up for every opportunity, stretched themselves too thin, and missed all the wonderful scenery that was passing by along the way. In an attempt to get ahead by speeding to the next level on their journey, they never caught their breath to reflect upon their accomplishments, big or small, and they never looked around to enjoy the view. They were anxious and darn near had heart attacks and strokes along the way to success. They were frazzled on their journey and never got to know themselves along the way because the destination of success was the only thing that mattered, not the journey. The speeder had one thing in mind: getting from point A to point B as rapidly as possible. The speeder must now change. Skill, patience, humility, deep breaths, appreciation for the journey, and a steady mind are needed to sustain this phase and get to the next level.

Rule-Breakers: Rule-breakers believe that running a red light and swerving in and out of traffic will shave a few minutes and get them ahead of others. They fail to realize that breaking the rules will eventually get them caught. The police will pull them over and take their precious time by giving them a citation and making them late, whereas had they followed the rules, they would have arrived at their destination in a better frame of mind and saved time, money, and frustration in the process.

These people think that because they were able to get away with breaking the rules in the past on their journey to success, they will somehow be rewarded by doing it again in the future. A series of short-term advantages brought about by breaking the laws of the road got them to their destination more easily than others. They hoped no one would notice along the way; however, the universe noticed. These individuals must quickly learn that the positive blessings from the universe manifest themselves only to those who follow its rules.

They may have been able to break the rules in the beginning, but the universe works to ensure that they will not get away with such acts in the end. In a constant state of inconsistency and recovery from the penalties associated with the choice not to follow the rules, their shortcuts in life will ultimately set them behind. The universe will kick them out of the success phase of their journey and place them right back in square one. The rule-breaker must now change. Skill, patience, humility, deep breaths, appreciation for the journey, and a steady mind are needed to sustain this phase and to get to the next level.

Drunk or Distracted Drivers: Even with a task as attention-consuming and critical as driving a two-ton guided rocket down a busy street, some drivers take this responsibility all too cavalierly. They drive intoxicated, send text messages, talk on the phone, put on makeup, blast their radios, and so on. Their minds are not on driving but, rather, on attempting to accomplish something other than driving, ultimately putting themselves and the lives of others at risk. Their laidback attitude toward the ramifications of not being focused on the task at hand disables them from competently executing their critical responsibilities.

To the distracted driver, there are other things that are more important than driving. Unaware of the world around them, these drivers use social interactions or an altered state of mind to avoid having to relate to other drivers on the road. They accidentally cut off other drivers or have near misses with pedestrians, completely unaware of the situation, while talking or laughing away, or dealing with an altered state of mind caused by intoxication.

On their journey to success, they used distractions like drugs, alcohol, and whatever else they could find to alter their state of mind to deal with day-to-day stresses. The drunk or distracted driver must now change. Skill, patience, humility, deep breaths, appreciation for the journey (though they probably cannot remember much of it on account of intoxication or inattentiveness), and a steady mind are needed to sustain this phase and to get to the next level.

Road-Ragers: Simply put, these people are dangerous. Sadly, we see elected officials and people on TV who proudly and publicly manifest characteristics similar to road-ragers. They are always in the right, and the rest of the world is always in the wrong. They believe that it is their duty to educate other drivers about how wrong they are and about how right they are entitled to be. Their narcissism empowers them with the false wisdom that other drivers are not allowed to make mistakes and that they are indeed perfect. They take their frustrations out on the world by cursing, cutting others off, getting revenge, pulling out guns, flipping others off, and venting their frustrations at every given opportunity. At best, their rage results in hurting the feelings of others; at worst, their rage results in the loss of life.

Just as in the journey of life, self-awareness and appreciation of fellow people in spite of their shortcomings are critical tools in managing the challenges that come on a daily basis. To protect yourself, deal very cautiously with road-ragers. Their lack of self-awareness and immaturity and their high levels of uncontrollable rage make life's journey all too challenging for themselves as well as for others who are in their presence. Being a royal jerk may have gotten road-ragers to the success stage, but they must immediately change. Skill, patience, humility, deep breaths, appreciation for the journey, and a steady mind are needed to sustain this phase and to get to the next level.

Are You Still Following the Rules of the Game?

Now that you are in the success phase, you have not forgotten about the rules, have you? Are you in this phase but trying to get to stability and happiness in your life by creating your own rules along the way? Are you a Speeder, Drunk or Distracted Driver, Road-Rager, or Rule-Breaker? If so, you are creating your own challenges and making it that much harder to get to a sustainable place of true inner joy.

Let this metaphor of the rules of the road apply to your personal and professional life as well as to the goals that you will have in the future. If you have these or similar habits and you choose not to change, you are setting up the universe to boomerang disappointment back at you. You will never get to your next destination in the frame of mind that you desire, which I believe for all of us should be true happiness. You have already achieved "success." Now isn't it high time that you started to appreciate it and do some things differently? Certainly you will enjoy your tremendous achievements a great deal more.

By making some changes and knowing that what got you here will not get you to the next level, you set up the universe to bless you with greater abundance, sustainability, and happiness.

Money is a mirror that reflects your strengths and weaknesses.

—*Dave Ramsey*

Just like a dangerous roadway, the world is full of uncertain social interactions, responses, and reactions. We never really know exactly who or what is around the corner. Mastery of one's mindset is a critical tool for survival and advancement, as well as stability and happiness. The driver who breathes deeply during conflict, acts decisively, executes without self-inflicted distraction, respects mortality, and communicates clearly is the one who will ultimately get to his or her next destination as safely and quickly as traffic conditions allow.

You have achieved your goals, but you have a long life ahead of you. Practiced powerful rituals on the road and in the journey of life will create an impenetrable shield that will protect you. Your peaceful state of mind will fertilize the seeds of happiness in your mind for years to come. Now breathe.

PURPOSEFUL MILLIONAIRE POWER PLAY

1. Self-awareness is the most important tool in the journey to self-mastery. Most drivers believe that they are good drivers. In fact, most believe they are the best drivers on the road. If this were the case, there would be no accidents. Take a moment to close your eyes and do the ninety-second breathing activity that you were taught earlier in this book. As you take deep cleansing breaths, reflect upon your habits and be absolutely honest with yourself. Are you a Speeder, Drunk or Distracted Driver, Road-Rager,

or Rule-Breaker on the roadways? Have you been a Speeder, Drunk or Distracted Driver, Road-Rager, or Rule-Breaker on your journey to success? Commit yourself to change immediately. Tell a trusted friend or loved one about your problem, and if necessary, seek help. Your life is at risk, and the lives of others are at risk. This honesty with yourself could save lives, and it could also make the destination of success all the more sweet for you.

2. The next time you are behind the wheel of a car, notice your breathing. Slow your breathing down by exhaling slowly and gently inhaling deep full breaths. Then begin to think positive thoughts about yourself and the cars around you. Obeying the traffic laws, notice how your anxiety levels are decreasing and that the world around you seems less dangerous. Begin to apply this breathing to your driving habits and notice how much less stressful driving becomes, particularly if you live in a big city ensnarled by traffic. If drivers cut you off, don't honk your horn or flip them off; simply breathe. By breathing and forgiving them, you regain control of the situation. Apply these driving habits and breathing exercises to your personal and professional life and notice how everything begins to change!

3. Repeat out loud five times, "I have everything that it takes to be healthy, wealthy, and happy. I am a Purposeful Millionaire."

CHAPTER SEVENTEEN

HAPPINESS IS NOT ELUSIVE— IT IS ALREADY HERE

If you want to live a happy life, tie it to a goal. Not to people or things.

—Albert Einstein

WHEN LOOKING TO the future, know that tomorrow is not guaranteed to be fun or to bring happiness and is certainly not promised to be easy. True happiness has to be earned and also honored. No matter what you gain in life or what is taken away from you, happiness is a ritual, a choice, and a frame of mind that cannot be taken away from you unless you allow it to be taken away from you. That is why happiness should be a daily goal for all of us, regardless of the circumstances in which we find ourselves or where we are in our careers or personal lives.

Something that truly baffles me is why so many people believe that putting off happiness today will prepare them for a life of happiness tomorrow. For example, most people toil through life showing up for a career (or marriage, for that matter) that they do not love so that they can build the nest egg they need to retire to a life of *perceived* happiness loafing alongside some beach somewhere. These folks do not think of work and life as an experience to be cherished, but rather, as a path to retirement. They have been miseducated about what happiness is. Something is wrong with these folks' journey to a destination of "happiness." This approach to cheating oneself out of an exciting and purposeful existence, over the majority of his or her best years in life, presents serious problems.

First, the best years of our lives are today. We will never be younger than we are today, so why wait until tomorrow to be happy, regardless of our career or financial circumstances? Next, if people are really unhappy in their present situations and cannot change their circumstances, shouldn't they use their mind as a free tool to find happiness?

What you get will never make you happy. Who you become will make you very happy or very sad, depending upon how you approach your life.

—*Anthony Robbins*

I have met many folks who, despite the humdrum nature of their jobs, are happy. Whether it was the hotel housekeeper whom I overheard singing beautiful hymns while cleaning or the school bus driver who greeted every child each morning as if it was his last day on earth, those people amaze me. They have created their happiness through the power of their minds, and equally as important they helped to make the world a little more joyful by sharing the beauty of their hymns or wonderfully pleasant attitude. Their joyful spirits make me and those with whom they come in contact smile. Their quiet acts enrich my life and yours too. They have problems and challenges that life throws at them just like everyone else, but they live in the present, not worried about the whims of tomorrow to put off the joys of today. There are a few ways I have found that work to get to that level of relatively consistent happiness. Let's explore them.

Rule #48: Work on yourself as much
as you work on your job.

As I have said before, because I don't want you to forget, the human brain is by a far measure the most powerful thing in the world. Period. It is the supplier of all innovation, communication, execution, and moreover, peace and happiness. It is also the single solitary supplier of judgment, prejudice, hate, greed, and war. It can be used to construct as well as to destroy. It is attached to our heads twenty-four hours a day, and whether we are at work or on a beach, it must be nourished and cared for with the right thoughts and beliefs.

Even while we are busy working, we can care for it simply by breathing and thanking the universe for the blessing of having enough work to pay the bills. Western society has a huge problem when in the words of Brené Brown, "We are the most in-debt, obese, addicted, and medicated adult cohort in U.S. history." This problem manifests itself in countless ways and could be prevented if more people knew how to care for their minds. Sadly, so many people live their entire lives without sitting through one free meditation session to get to know themselves better—or better yet, taking ten deep meditative breaths in the privacy of their own home or office to get their thoughts together so that they might better control the words that fly out of their mouths and the actions (or lack of action) that ensue.

I would guess that only a tiny percentage of the world's population actually practices any form of mindfulness, also known as getting in touch with the soul. The remaining vast majority of people in the world are asleep at the wheel of life and fail to let the greatest muscle they have—the mind—breathe fresh air. You can spot the small minority of mindful people across any room simply by looking at their smiles, their postures, and the positive energy that radiates from them like sunshine. Just imagine if all of our political and business leaders took just a few minutes a day to dig into their souls and thus guide their decision-making process based upon their inner peace. We would certainly have fewer wars and a lot less social inequity!

Practicing yoga has been one of the greatest tools in my mindfulness journey, as well as a secret weapon for professional and personal success. The meditative, slow breathing and movement all take me to a place of deeper introspection. When I finish up a morning yoga session whether it is in the studio at my home or in my hotel room, I know that the ritual of putting my mind first is a critical component to the level of happiness that I will be able to achieve that day. *Yoga* which is Sanskrit for "to connect" does exactly that for me: my mind, body, and spirit become connected through this practice. The small, incremental ritual of devoting time each day to it is a tremendous component to my life's trajectory and professional success.

With meditation and yoga, I am constantly evolving, getting to know myself at a much deeper level, and further awakening my consciousness and connectedness to the world. Also, no matter how many years I practice or how advanced I become, because I fall flat on my face from time to time during yoga, the universe reminds me to be humble and acknowledge that life is just a *practice* at which we strive to get better. This makes me a better person.

Let's say at worst that I am able to practice yoga thirty minutes every other day for one year. That turns out to more than five thousand minutes a year, or more than eighty hours a year that I dedicate to improving myself and nurturing my mind. Some people don't spend five minutes nurturing their minds in an entire lifetime—and it's obvious. We have business leaders and elected officials who could benefit from a serious dose of mindfulness. Because you are making changes in your life, becoming mindful and constantly becoming a better person, consider using this book as a tool to help you step up to the plate of leadership. This world needs you.

Just think about how much time people spend in front of the television looking at sports, instead of reading a book. Noam Chomsky, a world-renown philosopher, cognitive scientist, and social critic, once observed that when he listens to a sports call-in show, "It's plain that a high degree of thought and analysis is going into that. People know a tremendous amount. They know all sorts of complicated details and enter into far-reaching discussion about whether the coach made the right decision yesterday… These are ordinary people, not professionals, who are applying their intelligence and analytical skills in these areas and accumulating quite a lot of knowledge… On the other hand, when I hear people talk about, say, international affairs or domestic problems, it's at a level of superficiality that's beyond belief."

I love sports just like a lot of other Americans; however, I do know how to budget my time and stay focused on the personal ship that I am captaining. Chomsky's logic is abundantly clear: people invest their time in things with little to no meaning in the grand scheme of life yet are not willing to invest time, brainpower, and effort into analyzing their own lives or creating a path forward to harvest a more purposeful, fulfilling, and abundant life. They get lost in the details of a game that someone else is playing in and someone else is coaching—a game over which they have no control and can only view from the sidelines or the TV.

> Happiness is a work ethic. It's something that requires our brains to train just like an athlete has to train.
>
> —*Shawn Anchor*

A great competitive advantage for me in business and in life in general is this commitment to mindfulness. Perhaps yoga is not your thing, and something else works for you to achieve mindfulness. Whatever the case, do what is needed daily to turn within. The world will respond favorably. Happiness cannot be taken from you when you put yourself and your mind first. Happiness lies within you, not the world. No matter what is going on around you, you can be happy. If it's five below zero with three feet of snow outside and you hate cold weather, you can still be happy. If it's hot enough to boil an egg on a concrete sidewalk outside and you hate hot weather, you can still be happy. Take this commitment to being happy with you wherever you go—in the classroom, in the boardroom, on airplanes, in rush hour, and even in the bedroom. Wink, wink.

Rule #49: Set goals, but don't overdo it.

I am a firm believer in setting big, specific goals and working my butt off until I achieve them. However, everything does not always go my way. When something does not go my way or circumstances change and alter the course of my direction, it is critical to my happiness that I respond with flexibility and resilience. It is important to place a healthy amount of pressure on yourself but not to overdo it. Push yourself, but be gentle on yourself. Be kind to and forgiving of yourself. Failure to respond with flexibility and an open mindset to the blessing of the altered course of direction can create deep disappointment with the self, or in other words, misery.

Some people believe that the outcome of a goal is all that matters. That is simply not true. Being healthily unattached but completely committed to a goal is a great way not to set yourself up for heartbreak if the goal is not achieved. My faith has been important to me in the journey of being a business owner. When I have done all that I can to see a dream through and for one reason or another it does not come to complete fruition, I rest in the knowledge that my universe has a better plan in mind for me. This has always turned out to be true.

Indeed, as crazy as it may sound, I am grateful for each challenge that life throws at me. This gratitude during difficult times repositions the energy forces that are working in my life, and as such, an attitude of grief or ingratitude does not block me from noticing new golden doors of opportunity.

An attitude of gratitude for the good things and the bad (as well as the lessons learned from those challenges) positions me for a victorious life. Though I have no way of knowing exactly what the universe's plan is for me, incredible doors have opened for me that are the result of failure. The knowledge that the universe has a master plan for me, in tandem with a trained upbeat attitude and mindset of cool detachment from the outcome of my goals, has been the bedrock of my mental stability and the reason why I can continue smiling through the good times and the bad.

Rule #50: Don't confuse: 1) wealth with wisdom, 2) happiness with money, or 3) luck with skill.

Someone once said, "When you are poor, people pray for you. When you are rich, people listen to you." These words are true in so many ways, and society seems all too willing to take its cues from folks who are rich but lack wisdom (just think of the Kardashians). But even though society has a fascination with wealth and fame, happiness is often not part of the toolkit that automatically comes with financial abundance.

There are many people who are rich but unwise and even more people who are rich but unhappy, particularly those who became wealthy by money being handed to them or not having to go through true grit to earn it. Grit develops character; an interconnectedness with the universe; and a more honest valuation of one's skills, accomplishments, and luck, all of which lead to abundance. That is why it is important to focus on yourself, not on the glitter of others' fortunes or circumstances. Their wealth and perceived happiness may be fleeting while yours will be here to stay for the long haul.

Think of all the celebrities who have cracked before our eyes, living lives that are nothing short of drug- and drama-filled train wrecks, and sometimes paying the ultimate price for such a high level of dysfunction. Most people cannot handle the pressures of great wealth or fame on account of the major stressors and headaches associated with properly managing either one or, worse yet, both. People can stay for the long haul only at the level of wealth or fame that they can adequately handle. This stuff is really hard y'all, and many people have lost their lives trying to figure it out! That is why we cannot compare ourselves to others or put ourselves down.

> The superheroes in your mind... those might be idols, icons, titans, billionaires or whatever... are all walking flaws who have maximized one or two strengths. They succeeded because they knew their strengths. Everyone is fighting a battle that you know nothing about.
> —*Tim Ferriss, author of The 4-Hour Workweek*

A lot of folks could learn from the old truism that "It is none of my business what other people think about me!" I wonder how far each of us could go in life if every person had this attitude and approach toward managing toxic folks. To be truly happy, we need to be our own greatest personal cheerleaders and champions for living a spiritually healthy life of abundance. Also, we need to stop second-guessing the greatness that the universe has in store for each of us.

There will always be someone who is richer or more famous or better looking, so we have to consistently do the work that is required every day to achieve sustainable happiness. To do that, our minds must be nourished with the right fuel, which in turn creates the right attitude. Once the right attitude and mindset are locked down, blessings begin to pour in from all directions.

Rule #51: Pick the right medicine.
Happiness can be found in many different
ways—constructive and destructive.

Some people can find happiness exercising at the gym or running marathons to create a great physical body. Others find it with the fulfillment that comes along with achieving great career milestones. And others find it by spending precious time with family and friends. Unfortunately, some people find happiness in drug use, alcohol abuse, adultery, and other destructive—not constructive—habits.

Fortune does not change people; it unmasks them.

—*Suzanne Necker*

Each day, we have a choice. That choice is to be happy or not. However, each day we also have to prescribe the right good medicine to achieve that happiness. I have known financially successful people who are flat-out in a dark state of constant depression, while on the other hand, in spite of the challenges that each day brings them, I have witnessed the fulfillment and authentic happiness levels of other successful people skyrocket to levels that many people would deem impossible. The question then becomes: *what is the causative difference between happy and unhappy people?*

Money, if it does not bring you happiness, will at least help you be miserable in comfort.

—*Helen Gurley Brown*

The difference is mindset. A friend of mine is the heir to an incredibly successful private enterprise, and she struggles with constant doldrums of sadness. She and her children (and her grandchildren for that matter) will never have to worry about one penny for the rest of their lives. I asked her if she would speak with me about her feelings in life, and she agreed. She mentioned that even though she had every material blessing, she no longer found fulfillment in some of the things that other people found exciting or beautiful about life. She had traveled to dozens of different countries, flown on the finest jets, and dined with countless dignitaries; yet, all those privileges no longer excited her. She had gotten used to the lush life and no longer found any splendor associated with it.

So, I asked my friend what she was doing to ensure that she found fulfillment in her life. Was she involved in the right fulfilling philanthropic causes? Was she volunteering her time to assist the needy? Was she inviting into her various homes friends who were less wealthy but probably a lot more fun and less judgmental than stodgy rich people to experience her blessings with her? Was she afraid that someone would somehow take something from her, and thus avoiding having people around her? Was she active in her community, or was she exploring a new hobby or physical fitness challenge? Did she stick to a daily routine of exercise, meditation, work, and rest? These were a lot of questions, but the answers were all what I suspected. The problem with my friend's lack of happiness was that she was not picking the right medicine to remedy her suffering.

What worries you masters you.

—*John Locke*

Here's a problem: the more financially free people are, the more often they have been exposed to the adrenaline rushes of extraordinary experiences, and thus, the more challenging it is for some of them to find future excitement or fulfillment. Into the hearts of many, fear creeps in that someone will someday take something away from them, and therefore they become isolationists.

Unfortunately, at the highest level of professional ranks, cocaine and opioid abuse use is more common than it should be. Some senior executives, stars, and all-star athletes choose such drugs as their medicine to get a self-induced chemical high from life. In their minds, the high wakes them up—making them feel fully alive. It makes some of them feel loved. The high is an attempt to give them the rush that they first received when they cashed that first gigantic check, bought that first fancy car, or first heard the crowd chanting their name for an encore.

When people become numbed by the pressures of success, alcohol, cocaine, and other drugs are used as quick fixes to find happiness. If these individuals would spend as much time working on their subconscious as they do on their drug fixes, then true happiness, the kind that does not flee after a couple of hours, could be achieved. Happiness is a practice. Happiness is an ongoing practice that requires work, even when—especially when—one has already achieved success and wealth. It is better than any drug you can snort, inject, smoke, or drink. It is powerful, and best of all, it can be achieved legally, and often for free.

As you gain financial blessings, treat them just like that. As I have said, *blessing* is just another word for responsibility. Taking care of your mind first and choosing the right medicine to nurture your life will inevitably, like a magnet, bring the right kind of happiness, people, and opportunities into your life. Just do it.

Rule #52: You are the architect, construction crew, and maintenance team for your life. Just build it!

Nobody but you can create the life that you wish to live. No other person, other than our own self, is in charge of our journey and the decisions that we make. Everything we believe that we can do, we can; everything we believe that we cannot do, we cannot. Though not easy, life is much less complicated than many people make it.

When you create a great life and experience it to its fullest, it is a beautiful journey free of judgment, ignorance, and small thoughts—and full of love, compassion, focus, joy, perseverance, and abundance. Nothing reminds me more of this simple fact than the powerful words created by Holstee, a creative firm whose mission is to help people live a reflective and intentionally powerful life.

Holstee's "Manifesto" has become virally popular and is printed and distributed as artwork to thousands of homes and businesses annually.[2] At Excel Global Partners, to remind us of our mission and the decisions that we are in charge of, we reached out to Holstee, and they gave us permission to use their manifesto to begin and end our business strategy meetings. We cherish these words, both professionally and personally:

---

2   Permission to reprint received by Holstee.

THIS IS YOUR LIFE. Do what you love, and do it often. If you don't like something, change it. IF YOU DON'T LIKE YOUR JOB, QUIT. If you don't have enough time, stop watching TV. If you are looking for the love of your life, stop; they will be waiting for you when you start doing the things you love. Stop over analyzing, LIFE IS SIMPLE. All emotions are beautiful. When you eat, appreciate every last bite. Open your mind, arms, and heart to new things and people, WE ARE UNITED IN OUR DIFFERENCES. Ask the next person you see what their passion is, and share your inspiring dream with them. TRAVEL OFTEN; getting lost will help you find yourself. Some opportunities only come once, seize them. Life is about the people you meet, and the things you create with them so go out and start creating. LIFE IS SHORT. Live your dream and share your passion.

Happiness is certainly not elusive. It is achieved by exercising the mind, which is the greatest muscle there is. Improving your mind does not require a Herculean effort, but it does require that you not allow the saboteur of small thoughts and fear within your mind to control your destiny. People who allow the saboteur to control them will never achieve any of their dreams. But you will because you read this book, and each day forward, you will continue to work on mastery of yourself. This mastery of self simply requires consistent daily maintenance, focus, care, and self-love, and of course, the strength not to deviate from the rules in this book in all things that you do.

Over the course of time, you will see that application of our formula for success (Idea + Plan + Execution = Success) along with the rules in this book will add up to creating a purposeful life of abundance that you never imagined—and happiness will simply be the icing on the cake.

Review the rules in this book frequently and do the exercises, bringing them all into your deepest consciousness and permanent way of viewing the world. And if nothing else, as you set goals for your future, always follow the sequence: get the idea, create the plan, and spend most of your time executing your butt off.

PURPOSEFUL MILLIONAIRE POWER PLAY

1. Reflect upon Brené Brown's words: "We are the most in-debt, obese, addicted, and medicated adult cohort in U.S. history." What do her words mean to you? What do you believe they mean to the people closest to you? How can you immediately apply her words to change your spending, eating, and other habits? Talk about this quote with the five people with whom you spend the most time. Now that you are a Purposeful Millionaire who holds him or herself to a higher level of accountability, help them to change. Share this book with them, make sure they read it, and discuss it with them.

2. Reread the Holstee Manifesto. Is there anything that strikes you in particular? How did the manifesto make you feel? Write down the rule from the manifesto that most applies to your life right now. Write down what you will do to fix that part of your life going forward. Fold it up, place it in your wallet or purse, and pull it out wherever you are whenever you need encouragement.

3. Repeat out loud five times, "I have everything that

it takes to be healthy, wealthy, and happy. I am a Purposeful Millionaire."

4. Pull out your vision board and spend fifteen minutes in silence reflecting upon what you have envisioned for your future. Are you feeling inspired or overwhelmed? Embrace each feeling that comes to you. Think about the great possibilities of this world for you. Look at your board and say out loud:

"Happiness is expansion. This world is a place of infinite possibilities for me. My light, not my insecurities, has been what has made me most afraid. I love myself, and today, I forgive myself for not fully living up to my potential in the past. But I am now ready to share my light with the world. I promise that I will invest in myself on a daily basis and commit to rituals, habits, and an unrelenting consciousness that will empower me on the journey to developing my greatness. I already have everything that it takes to be healthy, wealthy, and happy. I will soon be a Purposeful Millionaire."

Repeat. Repeat. And repeat again throughout your life until your greatest potential is achieved. Welcome to the joys of being more purposeful, which can lead to the treasures of being a Purposeful Millionaire.

The choice is yours–and <u>only</u> yours.

MY PLEA TO YOU

NOW LET ME talk to you, person-to-person. Listen to me closely. You have made it to the end of this book; the time to act is now. Otherwise you just wasted your time reading it, and I wasted my time writing it. As a new member of The Purposeful Millionaire Club, you are now 100 percent in control of your future financial success as well as your happiness. No ifs, ands, or buts—you are in control, so don't let anyone rain on your parade or steer you in the wrong direction. People have no power over you now that you are the master of yourself.

I don't care if you were born under a rock, have purple skin, and don't have a penny to your name. You now know the rules of the game of success, so if you forget them or fall off track, pick this book back up and read it again! You are in complete control of your destiny, so unlearn and unpack all the pessimistic mental baggage that you have been carrying that has limited you and made you doubt your power.

Your mind is in control of your future. Take care of it. Nurture it. Strengthen it. If you care for it the right way, you can change not only *your* world but also *the* world. This world needs you to make a difference. Use this book as a tool to guide you in making that happen.

Never forget that not everyone has read this book. As such, you are now a member of a very special club of people, the Purposeful Millionaires, who know the formula for success *and* know that even fewer people are willing to get off their haunches and fully implement it. ***Idea + Plan + Execution = Success.*** You are a rare and unique person and, unlike others, you will ably apply this formula from start to finish until you achieve your audacious goal.

If you believe that you can become a Purposeful Millionaire, then just start doing it right now! Don't wait until next week, next year, or your next milestone birthday. Put the 52 rules into place right now and change your life. If you accept postponements and mediocrity in your life, that is exactly what you will get from others, including the universe. Be bold, dream big, and execute.

Write to me and send me pictures about your journey; visit me on social media and my websites at:

www.JamesNowlin.com

or

www.PurposefulMillionaire.me

Join The Purposeful Millionaire Club and connect with me on social media because nothing makes me happier than witnessing others find their calling, achieve their dreams, and create phenomenal success stories. Remember that you will never be younger than you are today and that if you wait on ideal conditions to present themselves, you will never get started—you will be like every other Tom, Dick, or Harry that talks about ideas and plans, but achieves neither. Note that Tom, Dick, and Harry do not have last names—they are forgettable characters. They are not standouts, and they are most certainly not purposeful. I know that you are not like them. *We* are not like them. My last name reminds me that every day I must live in the *now*. I am a *Purposeful* Millionaire who never takes no for an answer. A person who is going to execute his plan every day and ride this life on the high road until the wheels fall off. I have taught you what I know.

I will be rooting for you along the way and will plan on seeing you in the Success phase. Don't you dare disappoint yourself. The universe is waiting on you, and I am too.

Now just do it!

chapter, while remaining true to my voice. Thank you to Heather Habelka for her work on the back cover copy. Thank you to both Andrew O'Brien and Erin Schultz, my publicists whose respective rolodexes help to spread the wonderful message of our book across the world. And thanks to Rick Callahan for his contributions to getting our logo and website looking sharp.

My employees at Excel Global Partners, the EGP Family of Companies, and Excelerated Media, continue to amaze me. Their dedication, work ethic, and skills are first-class–I thank them for always having my back and for keeping the ship sailing forward.

To every great educator or academician who ever saw a special light in my eyes, I will always look up to you. You know exactly who you are. I will never ever forget you.

Thank you to the many millions of people in our nation who respect and celebrate excellence in business diversity, and to the wonderful organizations that unite us: National Minority Supplier Development Council, Women's Business Enterprise National Council, National Gay and Lesbian Chamber of Commerce, and United States Hispanic Chamber of Commerce.

To all of my clients, my friends in the world of book publishing, and to everyone who I have met on the road, at an airport lounge, in a hotel lobby, at a conference, or on social media, I thank you for the positive energy that you bring me. Being connected with you makes me purposeful and happy. Amen.

APPENDIX

Nowlin's 52 Rules for Creating a Life of Wealth and Happiness

Rule #1: First love yourself, and the universe will conspire to lift you higher. Your thoughts about yourself, money, and what other people think about you—and the way you respond to your thoughts—can build you up or completely tear you down.

Rule #2: Take the first step. You will never have an amazing journey if you do not take the first step, even if doing so scares the daylights out of you.

Rule #3: It is okay to feel that the world of opportunity has left you behind, but get over it.

Rule #4: Replace negative thoughts with radically positive affirmations.

Rule #5: To earn more, you must learn more! Knowledge creates empires. There is no substitute for knowledge. A lot of people pretend to be experts, but they are not.

Rule #6: Stop searching for someone to hand you the keys to success or to show you where they are. They are already in your hands. You just have to unlock the door of your mind.

Rule #7: Differentiate yourself as a true subject matter expert.

Rule #8: Always use your time wisely. It is an opportunity for you to apply your expertise. You are running out of time, and your life is much shorter than you think.

Rule #9: Always choose courage over comfort. Doing that takes an exceptional person. Exceptional people are different, and that is what makes them exceptional.

Rule #10: Spend the bulk of your time on executing your ideas, not on creating the perfect idea or on hashing out every imaginable detail of a plan.

Rule #11: Know that you are not in this game alone. You will certainly need other people, but more important, you will need to be able to call on your universe for strength throughout your journey.

Rule #12: You are your own best friend or your own worst enemy. Do not be your own greatest saboteur. Be your greatest cheerleader and muse in spite of what the world may have told you.

Rule #13: Realize that any way that you see yourself has been self-created.

Rule #14: Get your mind right, and your life will follow.

Rule #15: Never underestimate the power of freedom from debt.

Rule #16: Never count on your home to create wealth for you.

Rule #17: Always spend substantially less than what you make.

Rule #18: Use your money as a tool to advance your peace of mind. The true power of money is not about having things. It is about spiritual well-being and having options.

Rule #19: Envision your highest success.

Rule #20: If you are not willing to do the work, nothing will work.

Rule #21: Not everyone has the same dream, so tend to your own dream, and let other people live out their dreams. Focus on your plan and your plan only, and you will achieve exactly what you desire.

Rule #22: Whatever you create in your mind and stick to, however great or small, you will achieve.

Rule #23: For anything to be manifested in reality, it must first manifest itself in the mind.

Rule #24: Always have an attitude of gratitude. It is a magnet for future blessings.

Rule #25: Demonstrate the capacity to exquisitely care for your current blessings so that the universe will prepare more for you.

Rule #26: You must live and act in the *now* so that when opportunity presents itself, you can seize it.

Rule #27: Acting upon opportunity does not always end favorably. But when you fall, fall forward.

Rule #28: Allow your setbacks to open the biggest doors for your future.

Rule #29: Execution is nearly everything. Take the first step in spite of fear, and the universe will give you the courage that you need to continue each step of your journey.

Rule #30: Life is not always fair. Make it fair for you by accepting the rules of the game and acting upon them.

Rule #31: Prepare yourself for change as you climb the stairwell of social class. The differences between one social class and another and each one's rules of the game, subtle as they may seem, are tremendous.

Rule #32: Realize the extent to which your environment matters. You must realize that before you can accurately assess your own situation. Get the hell out if necessary.

Rule #33: Familiarity and comfort are overrated. Do not get trapped in a comfortable existence because nothing great is ever achieved in comfort.

Rule #34: Talent without application is a waste. Use your talent wisely.

Rule #35: Recognize your gifts, and make the sacrifices required to nurture and develop them fully.

Rule #36: Privilege and opportunity are underrated. Opportunity may bring comfort, but comfort will not bring opportunity.

Rule #37: Change Your Net-Work to Change Your Net-Worth: Always be busy expanding your network.

Rule #38: Always Show Up.

Rule #39: Understand the *Know, Like, Trust* formula.

Rule #40: Happy, lucky people surround themselves with happy, lucky people. Restrict your time with unhappy, unlucky people, including certain family and friends.

Rule #41: Discipline is the key to advancing talent. Without discipline, talent will never develop or create sustainable success.

Rule #42: Increase your talent in a compounding fashion, just as you increase your financial assets.

Rule #43: Use routine and daily habits to keep chipping away at your dreams. You will eventually create a beautiful sculpture.

Rule #44: To achieve goals, make sure that they are specific, measurable, attainable, relevant, and time-bound.

Rule #45: Money is our greatest currency other than love. When properly understood and handled, it compounds. Make your money compound by gathering it, growing it, and seldomly disturbing it.

Rule #46: Learn how to relax. You are in this game for the long haul.

Rule #47: Make your entire day important and relevant to your mission. You will never regain that time. How you spend your evening hours is just as important as how you spend your morning hours.

Rule #48: Work on yourself as much as you work on your job.

Rule #49: Set goals, but don't overdo it.

Rule #50: Don't confuse: 1) wealth with wisdom, 2) happiness with money, or 3) luck with skill.

Rule #51: Pick the right medicine. Happiness can be found in many different ways—constructive and destructive.

Rule #52: You are the architect, construction crew, and maintenance team for your life. Just build it!

LIST OF RECOMMENDED READINGS

Wallace Wattles: *The Science of Getting Rich*

Robert Greene: *The 48 Laws of Power*

Brendon Burchard: *The Charge, Activating the 10 Human Drives that Make You Feel Alive* and *The Millionaire Messenger*.

Charlotte Adler: *Time*, September 5, 2016. Ordinary Families. Extraordinary Kids. A Story of Nine Families.

Bob Proctor: *You Were Born Rich*

Napoleon Hill: *Think and Grow Rich*

David Schwartz: *The Magic of Thinking Big*

John Lee Dumas: *The Mastery Journal*

David Osborn: *Wealth Can't Wait*

George Fraser & Les Brown: *Mission Unstoppable*

Robert Kiyosaki: *Rich Dad, Poor Dad* and *The Cashflow Quadrant*

Paulo Coehlo: *The Alchemist*

ABOUT THE AUTHOR

James R. Nowlin is the Founder and Chief Executive Officer of Excel Global Partners and the Fund Managing Principal of the EGP Family of Companies. Excel Global Partners specializes in navigating companies through change and improving the financial and operational performance of corporations, governmental agencies, and non-profits around the world. Having completed engagements in fifteen countries and more than twenty states, the firm specializes in C-suite level executive coaching, as well as providing exceptional subject matter experts in finance & accounting, financial systems & information technology, and management consulting & corporate strategy.

James believes in positive daily habits encompassing a healthy mind, body, and spirit. His active life involves a dedicated yoga practice, bodyweight training, and trail-running. He adores rescue animals, including his forever ecstatic dog Cady who passed away from old age during the writing of this book, and his very fluffy cat named Conrad who is convinced that he is a dog. He and his partner's home base is in Austin, Texas. They can be found in Maui, Hawaii whenever their schedules permit.

For more information on Excel Global Partners, please visit:
www.ExcelGlobalPartners.com

For more information on James Nowlin, please visit:
www.JamesNowlin.com
or
www.PurposefulMillionaire.me